Positioning for Power

Kneeling low in prayer – standing tall in God

Stuart Robinson

Sovereign World

Sovereign World Ltd
PO Box 777
Tonbridge
Kent, TN11 OZS
England

Also by Stuart Robinson: *Praying the Price*

ISBN: 1 85240 228 8

This Sovereign World book is distributed in North America by Renew
Books, a ministry of Gospel Light, Ventura, California, USA. For a free
catalog of resources from Renew Books/Gospel Light, please contact your
Christian supplier of call 1-8004-GOSPEL.

Typeset by CRB Associates, Reepham, Norfolk
Printed in England by Clays Ltd, St Ives plc.

To Joe
who first alerted me to the fact
that God was planting another
book within me
and to Elizabeth and June
who worked so hard to produce
this manuscript ready for publication.

If you believe,
no proof is necessary;
if you don't,
no proof is sufficient.

(Underwood, Foote, Kalb and Stone
Is God Listening?)

Contents

Contents

Endorsement

Positioning for Power, written by my friend Stuart Robinson, is an excellent book that will help you tap into the power of prayer.

In prayer, we are changed forever, because prayer brings us into the presence of God. This book will help position you in practical ways to see a new release of God's power in your life. Read this book and be prepared to have the old wineskins of how you pray changed, and your faith increased as you witness answers to your prayers.

Peter Wagner
1998

Introduction

In Nigeria a regular monthly meeting brings together over 100,000 people to pray all through the night for revival. The event is held on a high site halfway along the main road between Lagos and Ibadan. It attracts so much attention and traffic chaos, that the Minister of Works threatened to close it down. But so many government officials attend the meetings that he had to think again. Nigeria has some of the fastest growing churches in the world – one church having over 100,000 members.[1]

Clearly these people prioritise prayer and are seeing some comparatively amazing results. But Nigerian Christians like their brothers and sisters in Korea, China, Argentina or wherever God is working, practice prayer power wherever they go.

Over 5,000 Christians have been meeting for whole nights of prayer for revival during 1997 and beyond in London. There are signs that God is answering their (and others) passionate pleas. The man behind this particular movement is Enoch Adeboye, a Nigerian pastor, who longs to see God do in the United Kingdom what he has been doing in Nigeria.[2]

Whether it's the sound of marching feet of 2,000 conversions per month at Brownsville, Pensacola since Father's Day 1995,[3] 150,000 converts in recent months in Bihar, India,[4] 25,000 converts a day in China[5] or explosive church growth in Lima, Peru,[6] it's always against a background of persistently powerful prayer.

While God's power is increasingly evident in many 'Third World' countries, much of the church of the Western World seems to be sputtering towards extinction. We are often overly distracted away from our basic mission into a labyrinth of preoccupations with liberation, feminist or postmodern theologies, not to mention our skirmishes with various forms of secular culture or just with other Christians.

Affluence allows for such leadership luxuries. 'But the people in the pews never forgot that they had come (to church) to pray.'[7]

Prayer is as natural to the Christian as flying is to a bird. However, Peter Wagner says, 'Not all prayer works, but effective prayer does. Powerful prayer works ... Prayer is powerful (but) some is equally impotent.'[8]

We all want to experience the power of God. We all want to pray, to see answers to prayer, to be effective and to see God's church grow.

This book will help not only to clean up some rusty spiritual terminals, but will also help you plug in with more certainty to some of God's power points.

Endnotes

1. 'Nigerian Press Report', quoted in *CWR Revival World Report*, May/June 1997, 3.
2. 'Redeemed Church of God Report', London, quoted in *CWR Revival World Report*, May/June 1997, 7.
3. The Internet
4. 'Heartcry for Asia', *Sowers Ministry*. Hong Kong, 1997.
5. *CWR Revival World Report*, May/June 1997, 12.
6. *Ibid.*, 10
7. Anne Underwood, Donna Foote, Claudia Kalb and Brad Stone, 'Is God Listening?' *Newsweek* (Australian Edition), 1 April 1997, 62.
8. C. Peter Wagner, *Prayer With Power*. Ventura, California: Regal, 1997, 14.

Chapter 1

Praying the Price

(Luke 11:1)

The famous scientist, Albert Einstein, was asked by a Princeton doctoral student in 1952, what was left in the world for original dissertation research? Einstein replied, '**Find out about prayer.**'

English pastor Sidlow Baxter, when he was 85 years of age, said:

> 'I have pastored only three churches in my more than 60 years of ministry. We had revival in every one. And not one of them came as a result of my preaching. They came as a result of the membership entering into a covenant to pray until revival came. And it did come, every time.' [1]

Former Chaplain of the United States Senate, Richard Halverson, advised that we really don't have any alternatives to prayer. He said:

> 'You can organise until you are exhausted. You can plan, program and subsidise all your plans. But if you fail to pray, it is a waste of time. Prayer is not optional. It is mandatory. Not to pray is to disobey God.' [2]

In the United States of America, at Larry Lea's Church on the Rock in Rockwall, Texas, numerical growth was from 13 people in 1980 to 11,000 people by 1988. When he was asked about such amazing growth, he said, 'I didn't start a church. I started a prayer meeting.'

When David Shibley, the minister responsible for prayer in that church was asked the secret of the church, he said:

> 'The evangelistic program of our church is the daily prayer meeting. Every morning, Monday through Friday, we meet at 5.00 am to pray. If we see the harvest of conversions fall off for more than a week, we see that as a spiritual red alert and seek the Lord.'[3]

In Korea, where the church has grown from almost zero to a projected fifty percent of the entire population in this century alone, Pastor David Yonggi Cho attributes his church's conversion rate of 12,000 people per month as primarily due to ceaseless prayer.

In Korea it is normal for church members to go to bed early so they can arise at 4.00 am to participate in united prayer. It is normal for them to pray all through Friday nights. It is normal to go out to prayer retreats. Cho says that any church might see this sort of phenomenal growth if they are prepared to '**pray the price. I pray and I obey**,' he says.[4]

Cho was once asked by a local pastor why was it that Cho's church membership was 750,000 and his was only 3,000 when he was better educated, preached better sermons and even had a foreign wife? Cho enquired, 'How much do you pray?' The pastor said, 'Thirty minutes a day.' To which Cho replied, 'There is your answer. I pray from three to five hours per day.'

Growth – A Supernatural Process

The church is a living organism. It is God's creation with Jesus Christ as its head (Colossians 1:18). From him life flows (John 14:6). We have a responsibility to cooperate with God (1 Corinthians 3:6). We know that unless the Lord builds the house we labour in vain (Psalm 127:1).

The transfer of a soul from the kingdom of darkness to that

of light is a spiritual, supernatural process (Colossians 1:14). It is the Father who draws (John 6:44). It is the Holy Spirit who convicts (John 16:8–11). He causes confession to be made (1 Corinthians 12:3). He completes conversion (Titus 3:5). It is the Holy Spirit who strengthens and empowers (Ephesians 3:16). He guides into truth (John 16:16). He gives spiritual gifts which promote unity (1 Corinthians 12:25), building up the church (1 Corinthians 14:12), thus avoiding disunity and strife which stunt growth.

This is fundamental spiritual truth accepted and believed by all Christians. However, the degree to which we are convinced that all real growth is ultimately a supernatural process and are prepared to act upon that belief, will be directly reflected in the priority that we give to corporate and personal prayer in the life of the church.

It is only when we begin to see that nothing that matters will occur except in answer to prayer, that prayer will become more than an optional program for the faithful few. Instead it will become the driving force of our churches.

Obviously God wants our pastors, other leaders and his people to recognise that only he can do extra-ordinary things. When we accept that simple premise, we may begin to pray.

In the Bible

The battle which Joshua won, as recorded in Exodus 17:8–13, was not so dependent upon what he and his troops were doing down on the plain. It was directly dependent upon Moses' prayerful intercession from on top of a nearby hill, with the support of Aaron and Hur.

In the Old Testament, not counting the Psalms, there are 77 explicit references to prayer.

The pace quickens in the New Testament. There are 94 references alone which relate directly to Jesus and prayer. The apostles picked up this theme and practice.

So Paul says, *'Pray continually, for this is God's will for you'* (1 Thessalonians 5:16).

Peter urges believers to be *'clear minded and self-controlled'* so that they can pray (1 Peter 4:7).

James declares that prayer **is** *'powerful and effective'* (James 5:16).

John assures us that *'God hears and answers'* (1 John 5:15).

In the book of Acts there are 36 references to the church growing. Fifty-eight percent (i.e. 21 of those instances), are within the context of prayer.

We would all love to see growth in every church in the world like it was at Pentecost and immediately thereafter. The key to what happened there is found in Acts 1:14 when it says:

> *'They were all joined together constantly in prayer.'*

They were all joined together – one mind, one purpose, one accord. That is the prerequisite for effectiveness. Then, they were all joined together **constantly** in prayer. The word used here means 'to be busily engaged in, to be devoted to, to persist in adhering to a thing, to intently attend to it.' The word is in the form of a present participle. It means that the practice was continued ceaselessly. In Acts 2:42 it says: *'They devoted themselves ... to prayer.'* In Colossians 4:2, Paul uses the same word again as a command: *'Devote yourselves to prayer.'*

Throughout history, the church has significantly expanded when Paul's command was obeyed.

In History

When we read the biographies of William Carey, Adoniram Judson, David Livingstone, Hudson Taylor and others, the initiating thrust of the work of their lives began in prayer encounters.

About a century ago, John R. Mott led an extraordinary movement which became known as the Student Christian Movement. It was based amongst college and university students. It supplied 20,000 career missionaries in the space of thirty years. John Mott said that the source of this amazing awakening lay in united intercessory prayer. It wasn't just that these missionaries were recruited and sent out in prayer; their work was also sustained through prayer.

Hudson Taylor, the founder of the China Inland Mission now known as Overseas Missionary Fellowship, told a story of a missionary couple who were in charge of ten preaching points. They wrote to their home secretary confessing their absolute lack of progress and they urged the secretary to find prayer intercessors for each place. After a while, in seven of those places, opposition melted, spiritual revival broke out and the churches grew strongly. But in three places there was no change. When they returned home on their next furlough, the secretary cleared up the mystery. He had succeeded in finding people to pray for only seven of the ten places. S.D. Gordon concludes, 'The greatest thing anyone can do for God and man is to pray.'[5]

The great reformers of previous centuries, Luther, Calvin, Knox, Latimer, Finney, Moody, all practised prayer and fasting.

John Wesley, the founder of what was to be known as the Methodist Church, was so impressed by such things that he would not even ordain a person to ministry unless he agreed to pray and fast at least until 4.00 pm each Wednesday and Friday.

These people seem to have discovered something which others of us are yet to learn. The more difficult the situation, the more we need to pray. And no time could have been more difficult than the eighteenth century.

Eighteenth-Century

During those years, France was working through a bloody revolution. Its leaders were declaring that the church was only a system of oppression for the human spirit. Karl Marx the founder of Communism would later agree. In France the Rights of Man had been declared in 1789. Christianity was being held in contempt. Demonic forces seemed to have been unleashed to drive the church out of existence. In many places in England preachers and people were pelted with stones if they dared to testify to Jesus Christ.

But in the 1740s, John Erskine of Edinburgh published a pamphlet encouraging people to pray for Scotland and elsewhere. Over in America, the challenge was picked up by Jonathan Edwards, who wrote a treatise called, 'A Humble Attempt to Promote Explicit Agreement and Visible Union of God's People in Extraordinary Prayer for the Revival of Religion and the Advancement of Christ's Kingdom.'[6]

For forty years, John Erskine orchestrated what became a Concert of Prayer through voluminous correspondence around the world. In the face of apparent social, political and moral deterioration he persisted.

And then the Lord stepped in and took over. On Christmas day 1781, at a little church in Cornwall, at 3.00 am, intercessors met to sing and pray. The heavens opened at last. They prayed through until 9.00 am and regathered on Christmas evening. Throughout January and February the movement continued. By March 1782 they were praying until midnight. No significant preachers were involved – just people praying and the Holy Spirit responding.

Two years later in 1784, when 83-year-old John Wesley visited that area, he wrote, 'This country is all on fire and the flame is spreading from village to village.'

And spread it did. The chapel which George Whitfield had built decades previously in Tottenham Court Road had to be enlarged to seat 5,000 people – the largest in the world at that time. Baptist Churches in Northampton, Leicester and the Midlands, set aside regular nights devoted to the drumbeat of prayer for revival. Methodists and Anglicans joined in.

Matthew Henry once wrote, 'When God intends great mercy for his people, he first sets them praying.'

Across the country prayer meetings were networking for revival. A passion for evangelism arose. Converts were being won – not through the regular services of the churches, but at the prayer meetings! Some were held at 5.00 am. Others were held at midnight. Some pre-Christians were drawn by dreams and visions. Some came to scoff but were thrown to the ground under the power of the Holy Spirit. Sometimes there was noise and confusion; sometimes stillness and solemnity. But always there was that ceaseless outpouring of the Holy Spirit. Whole denominations doubled, tripled and quadrupled in the next few years. It swept out from England to Wales, Scotland, the United States of America, Canada and to some Third World countries.

Social Impact

The social impact of reformed lives was incredible. William Wilberforce, William Pitt, Edmund Bourke and Charles Fox, all touched by this movement, worked ceaselessly for the abolition of the slave trade which came in 1807.

William Buxton worked on for the emancipation of all slaves in the British Empire and saw it happen in 1834.

John Howard and Elizabeth Fry gave their lives to reform radically the prison system.

Florence Nightingale founded modern nursing.

Ashley Cooper, the seventh Earl of Shaftesbury, came to the rescue of the working poor to end their sixteen-hour, seven-day-a-week work grind. He worked to stop exploitation of women and children in coal mines; and the suffocation of boys as sweeps in chimneys. He established parks, gymnasia, gardens, libraries, night schools and choral societies to be open to everyone.

The Christian Socialist Movement, which became the British Trade Union movement, was birthed.

The Royal Society for the Prevention of Cruelty to Animals was formed to protect animals.

Not only was there amazing growth in churches, but there was an astounding change in society because for forty years a man prayed and worked, seeing the establishment of thousands of similar prayer meetings, all united in calling on God for revival.

Missionary societies were also established which eventually affected many other countries. William Carey was one who got swept up in that movement. We speak of him as the 'father of modern missions.'

The environment of his situation was that he was a member of a ministers' revival prayer group which had been meeting for two years in Northampton in 1784–86. It was in 1786 he shared his vision of God's desire to see the 'heathen' won to the Lord.

He went on to establish what later became known as the Baptist Missionary Society. In 1795 the London Missionary Society was formed. In 1796 the Scottish Missionary Society was established, and later still the Church Missionary Society of the Anglicans was commenced.

Nineteenth-Century

That prayer movement had a great impact, but slowed down until the middle of the 19th century. Then God started something up in Canada. In America the necessity to pray was picked up in New York.

A quiet layman called Jeremiah Lamphier had been appointed by the Dutch Reformed Church as a missionary to the central business district. The church was in decline and the life of the city was somewhat similar. Lamphier didn't know what to do. So he called a prayer meeting in the city to be held at noon each Wednesday. Its first meeting was on September 23, 1857. Eventually, five other men turned up.[7] Two weeks later, they decided to move to a daily schedule of prayer. Within six months, 10,000 men were gathering to pray and that movement spread across America.

Surprise, surprise! Within two years there were one million new believers added to the church. The movement swept out to touch England, Scotland, Wales and Ulster.

Ireland was as tough a nut to crack as any. But when news reached Ireland of what was happening in America, James McQuilkin gathered three young men to meet for prayer in the Kells schoolhouse on March 14, 1859. They prayed and prayed for revival. Within a couple of months a similar prayer meeting was launched in Belfast. On September 21, 20,000 people assembled to pray for the whole of Ireland.

It was later estimated that 100,000 converts resulted directly from these prayer movements in Ireland.[8] It has also been estimated that in the years 1859–60, some 1,150,000 people were added to the church, wherever concerts of prayer were in operation.[9] Also old cross-cultural missionary societies were revived and new ones formed.[10]

Twentieth-Century

In the 20th century in the little country of Wales in October 1904 revival broke out. It was characterised by lengthy prayer meetings. In the first two months, 70,000 people came to the Lord.[11] Prior to this revival, one of its leaders, '... Evan Roberts prayed and interceded passionately for an outpouring of the Holy Spirit' for eleven years! [12]

In 1972 in the Enga Church in Papua New Guinea, there was a declining spiritual state. A few people committed themselves to pray. Then prayer meetings started amongst the pastors, missionaries, and Bible College students. Prayer meetings started in many of the villages.

And then on September 15, 1973, without any prior warning, spontaneously, simultaneously, in village after village as pastors stood to give their Sunday morning messages, the Holy Spirit descended bringing conviction, confession, repentance and revival.

Normal work stopped as people in their thousands hurried to special meetings. Prayer groups met daily, morning and evening. Thousands of Christians were restored and thousands of non-believers were converted. Whole villages became 100% Christian, and the church grew not only in size but in maturity.[13]

In the Philippines in the 1980s, as a result of some people attending an international prayer conference, 200 missionaries of the Philippine Missionary Fellowship each organised a prayer group daily at 7.00 am. They report that within a couple of years this directly resulted in the formation of 310 new churches.[14]

Over in Argentina amazing things are happening. Jose Luis Vasquez saw his church explode from 600 to 4,500 in five years. Hector Gimenez saw his church grow from zero to 70,000 in ten years. Omar Cabrera saw his church grow from 15 to 90,000 members in twenty years.

Those who have investigated this say that the major reason is because there has been consistent, powerful intercessory prayer.[15]

Wherever that principle is invoked, amazing things happen. In 1982 Christians in East Germany started to form small groups of ten to twelve persons, committed to meet to pray for peace. By October 1989, 50,000 people were involved in Monday night prayer meetings. In 1990 when those praying moved quietly into the streets, their numbers quickly swelled to 300,000 and 'the wall came tumbling down.' Prayer tumbles the toughest walls.

In 1981 in Thailand after extensive persistent prayer, the Hope of God Church was started by Dr Joseph Wongsak. By 1997, the movement grew to 18,000 people and planted over 700 churches in every district of Thailand as well as establishing 42 churches in various other countries. Prevailing prayer has remained central.

In Cuba in 1990, a pastor whose congregation never exceeded 100 people in a weekly meeting, suddenly found himself conducting twelve services per day for 7,000 people. They started to queue at 2.00 o'clock in the morning, and even broke down the doors just to get into prayer meetings.

Asked to explain this, Cuban Christians said, 'it has come because we have paid the price. We have suffered for the Gospel and we have prayed for many, many years.'[16]

When a group known as the Overseas Missionary Society saw that after 25 years of work in India all they could report was 2,000 believers in 25 churches, they adopted a new strategy. In their homelands they recruited 1,000 people committed to pray for the work in India for just 15 minutes per day. Within a few years the church exploded to 73,000 members in 550 churches.

In October 1995, after two and a half years of prayer, revival broke out in Brownsville, Florida in the United States. During the next 18 months, 90,000 people converted or re-dedicated their lives to God. The pastors attribute this remarkable movement to continued prevailing prayer. A feature of what is happening has been regular, persistent, large scale, weekly, corporate prayer.

Will we 'pray the price'?

Today there is great pressure from many directions in our society to work harder, to become smarter, to produce results, or to be moved aside. The church is also in danger of absorbing this mentality into its attitudes and practices, forgetting that success does not come by might nor by power, but by a gracious release of God's Holy Spirit (Zechariah 4:6).

Years ago, R.A. Torrey said:

'We live in a day characterised by the multiplication of man's machinery and the lessening of God's power. The great cry of our day is work, work, work! Organise, organise, organise! Give us some new society! Tell us some new methods! Devise some new machinery! But the great need of our day is prayer, more prayer and better prayer.' [17]

In many churches around the world there is now the most up to date, state of the art technology available to com-municate the Gospel. Yet frequently, comparatively little seems to be happening in so many countries.

In terms of the growth and mission of the church, could it be that while the world has learned to communicate with robots on Mars, in sections of the church we have forgotten to communicate with the Lord of the universe?

If that is so, then our best course of action is to stand again with the company of the first disciples and like them, return to the head of the church – Jesus Christ – and say, *'Lord, teach us to pray' (Luke 11:1).*

Endnotes

1. Bob J. Whillhite, *Why Pray?* Altamonte Springs, Florida: Creation House, 1988, 111.
2. David Bryant, *Concerts of Prayer.* Ventura, California: Regal Books, 1984, 39.
3. David Shibley, *Let's Pray in the Harvest.* Rockwall, Texas: Church on the Rock, 1985, 7.
4. John Peters, 'David Yonggi Cho Man of Faith'. *CWR Revival World Report,* November/December 1997, 13.
5. S.D. Gordon, 'Prayer, the Greatest Thing', *Australia's New Day,* April 1983, 40.
6. J. Edwin Orr, *The Eager Feet. Evangelical Awakenings 1790–1830.* Chicago: Moody Press, 1975, 14–15.
7. J. Edwin Orr, *The Second Evangelical Awakening.* London: Marshall, Morgan and Scott, 1955, 3–5.
8. *Ibid.*, 41–46.
9. *Ibid.*, 83.
10. Orr, *The Fervent Prayer.* 131.
11. J. Edwin Orr, *The Flaming Tongue. The Impact of 20th Century Revivals.* Chicago: Moody Press, 1973, 17.
12. Leonard Ravenhill, 'Give Me Children or I Die', *CWR Revival World Report,* May/June 1997, 11.
13. R. Seaton Arndell, 'Revival and Mission', *The Australian Baptist,* May 1990, 16, 46, 47.
14. Vonette Bright and Ben A. Jennings, *Unleashing the Power of Prayer.* Chicago: Moody Press, 1989, 22.
15. C. Peter Wagner, 'Spiritual Power in Urban Evangelism: Dynamic Lessons from Argentina', *Evangelical Missions Quarterly,* 27 April 1991: 132.
16. Greg O'Connor, 'Miracles in Cuba', *New Day,* May 1990, 7–9.
17. R.A. Torrey, *The Power of Prayer.* Grand Rapids, Michigan: Zondervan, 1974, 190.

Note:

Much of the material in this chapter comes from *Praying the Price* – published by Sovereign World – 1994.

Chapter 2

Why Pray?

(Matthew 6:5–8)

When Jesus was speaking to his disciples, three times he said: *'When you pray..., when you pray..., when you pray...'* (Matthew 6:5–8). Then he went on to give teaching on prayer. He did not say 'If you pray,' but 'when you pray...' It is not an option for the believer.

Whether we are rich or poor, learned or unlearned, mature or immature, old or young, we are all expected to pray. It is not something which is the exclusive province of preachers or pastors. It is the responsibility of every believer.

S.D. Gordon, the founder of the Christian and Missionary Alliance denomination, has said:

> 'The greatest thing that anyone can do for God and man is to pray. It is not the only thing; but it is the chief thing. The great people of the earth today are the people who pray. I do not mean those who talk about prayer; nor those who say they believe in prayer; nor yet those who can explain about prayer; but I mean those people who take time to pray.'[1]

When we look at the life of Jesus we find that regardless of the pressures upon him, his every activity seemed bathed in prayer.

> *'Very early in the morning while it was still dark, Jesus got up ... to pray.'*
> (Mark 1:35)

During a busy time:

> *'Jesus went out into the hills to pray and spent the whole night praying to God.'*   (Luke 6:12)

At a time of great success, we find him praying (Luke 5:15–16).

During a time of temptation, he is praying (Luke 22:39–46).

Elsewhere we find Jesus praying at a time of crisis, after the death of John the Baptist (Matthew 14:13).

Paul said that *'Jesus is at the right hand of God interceding for us'* (Romans 8:34). Imagine that, an intercessor's prayer meeting going on continuously for a couple of thousand years.

Whether on earth or removed from the earth, the strong picture we have of Jesus is as a person of prayer.

To his disciples he said, *'Watch and pray'* (Matthew 26:41).

Elsewhere he said, *'Always pray and never give up'* (Luke 18:1).

On one occasion Jesus affirmed that God's house would *'be called a house of prayer'* (Matthew 21:13).

Note, he did not say that the temple would be a place of teaching or preaching or a centre for social action. It was to be primarily a place of prayer. Obviously he regarded prayer as being absolutely foundational to any other activity that we might eventually carry out in his name.

The disciples followed on from the model and the commandments which Jesus gave to them. So they *'stayed continually at the temple praising God'* (Luke 24:53). In fact, they were constantly in prayer (Acts 1:14).

It was no wonder then that the winds and fire of Pentecost came to that group of believers and that thousands were converted. They were tapping into the power of God through prayer.

Down through the decades of Christian ministry, as recorded in the Bible, that trend continued. So the apostle Paul later said, *'Pray continually'* (1 Thessalonians 5:17).

He went on to say:

> *'Pray on all occasions ... with **all** kinds of prayers and requests ... **always** keep on praying ... for **all** the saints.'*
>
> (Ephesians 6:8)

Paul followed his own advice. Writing to his friend Epaphras, he says that he was one who was *'always wrestling in prayer'* (Colossians 4:12).

There are the example and the commands of our Lord, the example of the disciples, the early church, the apostles, their teaching and their commands. They lived out what they preached. It would seem then, that this is something which is important for effective Christian living. The question is – **Why is it so?**

There are many reasons given in the Bible as to why we should pray. Let's look at just three which are foundational to so many other issues.

1. Fellowship with God

Firstly, we pray because in this way we have fellowship with God through the Holy Spirit.

Mostly when we think of prayer, we do so with ourselves at the centre of the universe of our own needs. We think of asking, getting and receiving. Furthermore, if we do not get what we ask for, and that right quickly, we tend to feel that prayer doesn't work. We judge it as a waste of time.

It is legitimate to ask and often we do receive. But more importantly than how I feel or what happens to me in prayer, is how does God feel?

The Bible says that *'God is love'* (1 John 4:8). If we ever doubt that, we need merely to remind ourselves that God so loved us and the entire world, that he sent Jesus to die in our place to accept the penalty and the burden of our sin, so that we might be free once more to enjoy fellowship with him (John 3:16; Romans 5:8).

But love cannot exist in isolation. It has needs to be met. It wants to be in the presence of the object of that love. Lovers must spend time together or else love suffers, dries and dies.

In that God is love, he has an unquenchable desire to have fellowship with his children. We are created in his image for him to have fellowship with us, to satisfy his father-heart. Any needs which we have ought to be subordinated firstly to fulfilling needs which God has.

So prayer is not to be considered as just rushing to a set location at a fixed time each day to race through some list of mentionable items. It is a relationship with God where we open ourselves to him and spend time in his presence.

The essential ingredient in building any relationship is time spent in the presence of the other. If we spend little time with God, then we will accomplish little in him. Consistency in our prayer life is evidence of the true depth of our commitment to him. For the time we give to him speaks much more than whatever it is we might try to accomplish for him.

If we seldom talk to or listen to God, then in effect we are telling him he has only a secondary place in our lives. Apostasy, dryness, barrenness, and powerlessness usually begin by our failure to spend time in prayer.

To the best of my recollection, I have never met anyone who has fallen away from a relationship with God, who has a life of constant prayer. This is because the believer who 'prays without ceasing' is usually one who is going on from strength to strength – rejoicing.

In this process, when we pray we give our Lord access to our needs. We allow him to relieve us of our distress. He reminds us that when we ask for bread he will not give us a stone (Luke 11:11–12). He says that when we ask, seek and knock, we receive and we find doors open (Matthew 7:7–8).

Because we open ourselves to him to allow a relationship to develop, then like luminous watch faces exposed to the sun:

> 'We are being transformed into his likeness with ever increasing glory.'   (2 Corinthians 4:18)

So the first reason for prayer is to have fellowship with God.

2. To Bind Satan

A second reason to pray is that in this way Satan may be bound on the earth.

Jesus said:

> *'Watch and pray so that you not fall into temptation.'*
>
> (Matthew 26:41)

The apostle Peter said:

> *'Be self-controlled and alert. Your enemy the devil prowls around like a roaring lion looking for someone to devour.'*
>
> (1 Peter 5:8)

Satan is cunning. He is mighty. He is powerful. He never rests. The Bible reminds us that, *'even the archangel Michael, when he was disputing with the devil about the body of Moses, did not dare to bring a slanderous accusation against him, but said, "The Lord rebuke you!"'* (Jude 9).

If the archangel Michael had so much respect for Satan, then we also need to be very careful in what we do in this realm.

In writing to the church at Ephesus, the apostle Paul said:

> *'Our struggle is not against flesh and blood, but against the rulers, against the authorities, against the powers of this dark world and against the spiritual forces of evil in heavenly realms.'*
>
> (Ephesians 6:12)

In the light of this, he urges us to *'put on the full armour of God so that when the day of evil comes we may be able to stand'* (Ephesians 6:13). He concludes his urging of us by saying:

> *'Pray in the Spirit on all occasions with all kinds of prayers and requests ... Be alert and always keep on praying for all the saints.'*
>
> (Ephesians 6:18)

In the western world, many Christians have no trouble believing that there is demonic activity in less (economically) developed countries. They believe the people who come from those countries and tell stories of encounters with the demonic. But many Christians in the west no longer believe that such things are possible in their own countries.

They have the false idea that because we are supposedly developed or 'civilised', that Satan is no longer interested in us. Many in fact, no longer believe that there are demons or even Satan. He undoubtedly is very happy with their holding to that false belief.

On the other hand, many who do believe the whole Bible, rather than just parts of it, never turn up to practise what they preach. They are in the army of the Lord, but never turn up for the roll call. They treat these things as if it's someone else's responsibility, or it's too difficult, or as if it belonged only to certain sections of the church.

If we read our newspapers and magazines or watch the television news, it is quite obvious that the only way we can explain many of the things which come before us is through the existence of wide-spread, personalised evil in the world. Even the secular magazine, *Time*, tended toward that conclusion in one of its cover articles.[2]

We need however not just to believe in the existence of evil, but to practise that which stands against it. We need to take up our weapon of prayer, for only then will Satan be bound and defeated.

In western countries there is a very well-known book called *The Screwtape Letters*, written by a professor who was at Oxford University in England. His name was C.S. Lewis. The book records in story form, imaginary conversations between a senior demon, Screwtape, and a junior demon, Wormwood. In one place Screwtape comments on the need to prevent prayer at all costs. He says, 'The best thing, where possible, is to keep the (Christian) from the serious intention of praying altogether.'[3]

When we pray we exert a positive influence upon the hosts of evil. They fear it and they fear those who become skilled in its use.

In 1958 Pastor David Yonggi Cho of Korea, went out to establish his first church in a small village in which there was a non-Christian temple. When he had pitched his tent, the high priest and followers of that temple went to him and said, 'You can't start a Christian church in our town without getting our permission and we won't permit you to come into this town.'

Pastor Cho stood his ground and refused to depart. So the priest replied, 'You are a dead person. You will never leave this town alive.'

To which Pastor Cho replied, 'You can't kill me. I am coming in the name of Jesus Christ.'

Here was a classic power confrontation with evil.

As Pastor Cho preached night after night, Satan's messengers came and threw rocks at him and tore down his tent church. Finally they came and said,

> 'You have been preaching that your God is a living God who heals. Down in that nearby village there is a woman who has been paralysed for seven years who has given birth to a girl. Both of them are dying. If you can cause her healing within thirty days, you may start your church here, otherwise you are out!'

Pastor Cho went to the village, visited the home and saw this starving, stiff, paralysed woman with her weakened child. The room stank with human excrement.

As an opening move in this spiritual warfare, Pastor Cho tried to lead her to Jesus Christ. She replied, 'I don't need Jesus. If you want to do anything for me, strangle me and kill me.'

Next Pastor Cho went and cleansed the room, changed the clothes, and made some beef soup. He fed the woman and then commenced to fast and pray himself. He prayed throughout the remainder of the thirty days. Toward the end, in desperation, he cried out, 'God, you've got to help me! In the name of Jesus Christ I bind this devil.'

Then he fell down into a trance and had a vision in which he heard very strange music. In the vision, suddenly his door was opened and there was a beautiful big snake with the head of a human, standing on its tail, dancing in time with the music. It came to him and said, 'If you don't move out of this town, I am going to kill you.' To which Pastor Cho replied, 'I'm not moving.'

A battle followed for three hours. Cho knew that he was losing as the snake swirled nearer and nearer to bite off his head. With his last ounce of strength, almost paralysed himself, Cho breathed out the word, 'Jesus'. He reports,

> 'Suddenly, I saw fear appear in the eyes of the devil. With all my strength I repeated the words "Jesus, Jesus, Jesus". The devil became powerless and slumped down. I put my heel on his head and crushed him. I walked out of my room with that dead snake in my arms and said to all of the people of the town who were gathered – "Look! You've been serving this snake all this while!"'

The vision finished. Pastor Cho returned to consciousness. The next morning he went to his early morning prayer meeting. By the end of that time, most of the town had turned out and were moving toward the church. Cho thought that they were coming to burn it down. Instinct told him to run away, but he determined to meet them face to face.

As he stood there, he saw that the crowd was being led by a young woman carrying a baby. On her face was a beautiful smile. As she drew closer he noticed that her face was almost exactly the same as that of the lady who was dying of paralysis and he wondered if they were twins.

'Who are you?' Pastor Cho said. The woman replied,

> 'Pastor, last evening at 2.00 am you came to the yard of my house. You shouted to me, "Rise up and walk in the name of Jesus!" I was in so much pain and because you were shouting I couldn't sleep so I rose up, and suddenly I felt power pouring into my limbs. I was healed and when I lifted my baby, the baby was whole also!'

As Pastor Cho had been wrestling in his room, so the Lord had done that special work. The people were now not marching out to destroy the church, but to celebrate the

powerful name of Jesus. This lady was jumping and praising
God.

On that site there is now a church which seats 5,000
people.[4]

When we pray, Satan will be bound.

Even the weakest Christian can inflict a great wound on
Satan by use of the lethal weapon of prayer.

3. Experience the Kingdom

Thirdly, when we pray enjoying fellowship with God and
binding Satan, then we experience the kingdom of God.

According to the record of the baptism of Jesus, it says that,

> *'As Jesus was praying, heaven was opened. The Holy Spirit
> descended and a voice came from heaven saying, "You are my
> Son whom I love."'*
> (Luke 3:21–22)

As Jesus was praying, as he was submitting himself, as he
was affirming his dependence on and expressing his faith in
his heavenly father, then the heavens opened, the Spirit
descended, the voice of God boomed forth. As we pray, the
heavens may open. God reveals himself. He talks with us. A
relationship is established.

The Bible says that:

> *'The prayer of a righteous man is powerful and effective.'*
> (James 5:16)

It is prayer not program which is powerful and effective,
because that prayer unleashes God's sustaining power.

About a century ago American evangelist D.L. Moody was
invited to preach at a church in the north of London. He
reported that as he preached he had neither power, nor
liberty. It seemed to him as if he was pulling a heavy train
up a steep grade. As he preached he said to himself, 'What a
fool I was to consent to preach!'

He tried to be released from preaching in the same church
that night. But the pastor of the church persisted. As Moody
preached that night it seemed to him that all of the powers of

the unseen world had fallen upon that audience. He drew his message to a close as quickly as he could and invited those who wished to accept Christ to stand.

About 500 people stood to their feet. Moody thought they must have been mistaken, so he told them to sit down and went through the procedure again, then instead of telling them to stand, he asked them to meet with the pastor in a room off to the side of the church. So many streamed out that they could not get into that smaller room. So Moody thought there must still be a misunderstanding. He gave instructions again that for those who really meant to receive Christ, they were to come back the following night.

Moody left for Ireland the next day, but revival broke out in the church and flowed out into other churches. What was the reason for the change between the unfruitful morning and the outpouring of the Spirit in the evening?

Moody himself reported that he had discovered that there were two sisters in that old church, one of whom was bedridden. The other one had heard Moody preach that Sunday morning. She went home and said to her sister, 'Who do you suppose preached for us this morning?' The sister replied, 'I don't know.' 'Mr Moody of Chicago was the preacher,' she was told.

No sooner had she said that when her invalid sister replied,

> 'What! Mr Moody of Chicago! I've read of him in an American paper and I have been praying that God would send him to London and send him to our church. If I had known that he was to preach this morning I would have eaten no breakfast; I would have spent the whole morning in prayer and fasting. Now sister, go out, lock the door, do not let anyone come to see me. Do not let them send me any dinner. I am going to spend the whole afternoon and evening in fasting and prayer!' [5]

And so the power of heaven descended.

If God could use a bedridden invalid saint like that, then he can certainly use any of us. It doesn't matter to what church we might belong, or whoever the pastor might be. God's power is unleashed if we will give ourselves to prayer.

When R.A. Torrey took over Moody's church in Chicago, he found that the main reason that church was so powerful, the main reason for it being packed Sunday by Sunday with conversions every week, was that men and women sat up late Saturday night or rose early Sunday morning to pray for their pastor. And the story of every great person in God is the same.

It is not so much the pastors who are preaching, but the people who are behind them praying which accomplishes great things for God.

A man by the name of Charles Finney was greatly used of God along America's eastern states in the first half of the nineteenth century. Much has been written of him, but very few know of an old man called Father Nash who would precede Finney to the cities scheduled for his meetings.

Three or four weeks in advance of the meetings, old Father Nash moved quietly into the town and found a place to pray. Relentlessly he prayed on. Finney's name gained in fame. His sermons pierced the hearts of the multitudes. But somewhere kneeling alone, there was always humble Father Nash.

At the conclusion of each series of meetings, old Father Nash moved on to labour on bended knees on the next battle front. He had no home, no church support and often missed the taste of home cooked meals. What did Nash receive for all of this? He received little in his lifetime, perhaps. But, the effects of his prayer were seen in the lives of $2\frac{1}{2}$ million people that Finney was used to bring into the kingdom of God. Every Finney needs a Nash to release the powers of heaven through ministry.[6]

Conclusion

If God is the one who hears and answers prayer, then let us pray! It becomes our most compelling privilege.

God never commanded us to sing without ceasing. God never commanded us to preach without ceasing. God never commanded us to give without ceasing, or to work without ceasing. But he did command us to pray without ceasing.

When King Solomon of Israel built the temple at Jerusalem and dedicated it to God, God did not say he would be listening for the songs of choirs. He did not say he would be looking for the smoke of the altars where many sacrifices were to be offered.

But he did say,

> *'Now my eyes will be opened and my ears attentive to the prayers offered in this place.'* (2 Chronicles 7:15)

May he increasingly hear prayers offered from every nation and every place that acknowledges Jesus as Saviour and Lord, as we all:

- develop fellowship with him;
- bind Satan; and then
- increasingly experience the kingdom of God coming to earth.

And as he hears us may we also be able increasingly to hear him.

Endnotes

1. Dick Eastman, *No Easy Road*. Grand Rapids, Michigan: Baker Book House, 1971, 16.
2. Lance Morrow, 'Evil', *Time*, June 10, 1991, 46–51.
3. C.S. Lewis, *The Screwtape Letters*. New York: MacMillan, 1969, 24.
4. David Yonggi Cho, 'My 30-day Battle with Satan', *Dawn Report*, August, 1995, 3–5.
5. R.A. Torrey, *The Power of Prayer*. Grand Rapids, Michigan: Zondervan, 1974, 37–38.
6. Wesley L. Duewel, *Touch the World Through Prayer*. Grand Rapids, Michigan: Francis Ashbury Press, 1986, 83–84.

Chapter 3

What to Pray

(Matthew 6:5–15)

Speaking on the prayer life of Jesus, E.M. Bounds said that 'Prayer was the secret of Jesus power. It was the law of his life, the inspiration of his toil, the source of his wealth, his joy, his communion and strength.' It was also the necessity of his life and because of this Jesus could say 'I always do what pleases my Father' (John 8:29).

To his disciples Jesus said, *'Watch and pray'* (Matthew 26:41).

Because of what his disciples saw Jesus doing, they came to him one day and said, *'Lord, teach us to pray...'* (Luke 11:1).

And isn't this the same question for many of us still? 'Lord, teach us to pray.'

Jesus answered his disciples by giving them what today is known as The Lord's Prayer. It would be better called The Disciples' Prayer. Prayers that Jesus actually prayed are recorded elsewhere. This one he gave to us to pray.

The event in which it was given is found in Luke 11. But what he gave them on that day was also taught two years earlier (Matthew 6:9–13). These teachings give a good guide as to what should be the outline and content of our prayer.

However, one of the problems we face in considering what is commonly known as The Lord's Prayer is that it has been so often repeated as a part of church worship services that it has lost much of its deeper significance and meaning. Our very familiarity with it has anaesthetised our minds and dulled our emotions so that we no longer spontaneously respond to the depths of its meaning or to the charge of its words.

Be that as it may, our Heavenly Father himself is recorded as saying:

> *'This is my son whom I have chosen; listen to him.'*
>
> (Luke 9:35)

Therefore again we must listen to the very words of Jesus if we want to learn how and what to pray.

1. Presence of God

Jesus started his teaching by saying,

> *'This is how you should pray: "Our Father in heaven hallowed be your name ... " '* (Matthew 6:9)

The first thing we need to note is that Jesus draws attention to the presence of God.

He does not say, 'My Father' but 'Our Father'.

With that we are lifted up from out of ourselves and more intimately toward God. When we say 'Our Father' we are reminded that we are not praying alone. We are praying together with all other men and women who have been and are alive in him.

That word 'our' puts us in the right context. The word 'Father' points us in the right direction.

The word 'Father' comes from an Aramaic word *'Abba'*, which loosely means 'Daddy'. This of course, was a familiar homely title used in the language of Jesus' time. When religious leaders of the day heard of it they were deeply shocked that anyone could consider their relationship with God in such terms. We ought never to forget the tremendous privilege of being able to call God 'Our Father'. Today we accept it without question. When Jesus used it he was almost stoned to death on the spot. If it was not for him, we would never have been able to use this title for God.

The Bible says:

> *'But when the time had fully come, God sent his son born of a woman, born under the law, to redeem those under the law that we might receive the full rights of sons.'*
>
> (Galatians 4:4–5)

That privilege is extended even further:

> *'For you did not receive a spirit that makes you a slave again to fear but you received the spirit of sonship and by him we cry, "Abba, Father." The Spirit himself testifies with our spirit that we are God's children. Now if we are children then we are heirs, heirs of God and co-heirs with Christ . . .'*
>
> (Romans 8:15–17)

The apostle John exclaims with amazement,

> *'How great is the love the Father has lavished upon us, that we should be called children of God!'*   (1 John 3:1)

'Our Father' implies a close, intimate, living, endearing relationship and when we pray to him we need to keep in mind that we are praying to a living and a loving God who is present and who loves us. To call him 'Father' means that we identify with what we are – his children. A father is he who has given life to his children, who communicates without misunderstanding with his children.

As we pray we need to understand the fact that God is primarily our father. If we can grasp hold of that it can change our lives. It will not be enough to accept that he is 'Father' without putting aside time to allow a relationship to develop with him so that he can become a truly loving father.

I obviously had a biological father. Everyone does. But, for the first four years of my life we spent little or almost no time together, because he was absent, serving in our nation's Air Force during the second World War. I knew about him but I didn't know him. We could not develop a relationship because we could not spend time together.

Similarly, knowledge about God is never enough. Experience of his loving us is what changes us. That happens as we allow time to come before him, to open up our conversation with 'our Father'. In this way we identify ourselves as being his children who are totally dependent upon him for all things.

When Jesus said it was difficult for a rich person to enter into the kingdom of God he was speaking truth. Rich people think they have no needs. They are not dependent on anyone or anything. If a need arises they throw money at it to solve the problem. They find it very difficult to acknowledge dependence upon another. But this is exactly what it is to be like if we are children of God. We enter into his kingdom as totally dependent children as much as our children on earth are dependent upon those of us who are parents.

Bilquis Sheikh in her biography, *I Dared to Call Him Father*, tells how she was born into a conservative Muslim family. Her husband had served as Pakistan's Minister of the Interior. She was restless in her search for spiritual reality. So she ordered her chauffeur, who was a Christian, to bring her a Bible. Occasionally she read from both the Bible and the Koran side by side.

She once confided to a Christian worker, 'I'm confused about your faith. It seems to make God so personal.'

To which the lady replied, 'Why don't you talk to God as if he was your father?'

Bilquis Sheikh recalls going to her bedroom, getting down on her knees and trying to call God, 'Father'. But afraid that it might be sinful to try to bring God down to her level, she dared not and gave up. However later that night she got out of bed, got onto her knees and called out 'Father!' She continues:

'Suddenly that room wasn't empty any more. God was there. I could sense his presence. I could feel his hand laid gently on my head. He was so close that I found myself laying my head on his knees like a little girl sitting at her father's feet. For a long time I knelt there sobbing quietly and floating in his love. I found myself talking with him and apologising for not having known him before.'

After a time she reached to the bedside table where she kept the Bible and the Koran. She lifted one book in each hand and said, 'I am confused, Father. Which one is your book?'

Suddenly she heard a voice inside her that said to her as clearly as if she was repeating words from her own mind, 'In which book do you meet me as father?' The Bible was his book and it was in her own hands.[1]

When we say *'Our Father in heaven, hallowed be your name'* we enter into the very presence of God.

Secondly we come to the **priorities** of God.

2. Priorities of God

Jesus said:

> *'Your kingdom come, your will be done on earth as it is in heaven.'* (Matthew 6:10)

In a kingdom the king is the sole one in charge. God desires that his kingdom is established through his children here and now. He waits to work his will on earth in answer to what we humans ask. But the nature of his character is that he chooses to rule only where invited, where those who desire his will to be done declare it to be so.

When we pray, 'Your kingdom come, your will be done . . .' that means that we are praying that our will shall be undone. It means that we are surrendering our wills and accepting God's will as the only authentic authority over us. His will is to be expressed not just over us individually but over our families, the church, the nations and all world rulers.

When we pray, 'Your kingdom come' we are making a faith declaration that nobody is going to rule but Jesus and that we seek nothing but his order, his power and priorities, his justice, his mercy, unity and love. To pray 'Your kingdom come,' means that we refuse to have any areas of our lives remain under our control and that we hand over our hands, our feet, our finances, possessions, plans, family, friends, location, reputation, the whole of our lives to him.

It means that we take on a kingdom mentality and start to walk in kingdom authority and power and that we expect demonstrations and revelations of God's kingdom to flow through us.

'Your will be done on earth as it is in heaven.'

Whenever we pray that it means that, we are lifted out of ourselves and are opting for God's priorities. This saves our prayer from becoming merely a printout of our self-interests.

Having established that we will live according to God's priorities we can expect thirdly, the **provision of God**.

3. Provision of God

Matthew 6:11 says:

'Give us today our daily bread.'

While we need to be careful to be praying in God's priorities, remember that one of his priorities is that our daily needs should be met.

Our heavenly Father promises that he will clothe us and feed us (Matthew 6:25–34). Children have no inhibitions about asking their fathers to meet their needs. We ought not to be backward about coming forward to God to ask him to meet our legitimate needs. Asking is a rule of God's kingdom.

Jesus said:

'I will do whatever you ask in my name so that the son may bring glory to the Father. You may ask me for anything in my name and I will do it.' (John 14:13–14)

Later on Jesus adds:

'I tell you the truth. My Father will give you whatever you ask in my name. Until now you have not asked for anything in my name. Ask and you will receive and your joy will be complete.' (John 16:23–24)

In asking however, remember we cannot become receivers unless we are also givers. To such God pours out his abundance because he knows he can trust them.

Also remember in asking we should not content ourselves with generalities. We need to pray in terms of specific needs.

Kenneth Ware and his French wife were forced to leave France and to relocate to Switzerland because of their wartime activities in hiding Jews from Nazis. On one occasion there was no food in the house and there was no money to purchase provisions.

Mrs Ware prayed in utter simplicity,

> ' "Jesus, I need five pounds of potatoes, two pounds of pastry flour, apples, pears, a cauliflower, carrots, veal cutlets for Saturday and beef for Sunday." She even told God the brand of flour she preferred. After listing her requests she said, "Thank you, Jesus." '

At 11.30 am that same morning a radiant faced blue-eyed blonde man wearing the customary long blue apron of a delivery man for that part of the world, called at the door and said in perfect French without any Swiss accent, 'Mrs Ware, I am bringing you what you asked for!'

Both Mr and Mrs Ware protested that there had been some mistake. But the delivery person persisted, 'I am bringing you what you asked for.'

Then he emptied the grocery basket placing on the table the exact items, neither more nor less than Mrs Ware had talked to God about right down to the exact brand of flour. Then he left.

Mr Ware completes the story,

> 'There was only one way for that delivery man to pass and that was before the window where I was standing but though I watched and Mrs Ware opened the door again to examine the hallway he was gone. There was no trace of the delivery man anywhere.'[2]

Are we surprised by that story? Why should we be? Didn't Paul say,

> *'Do not be anxious about anything but in everything by prayer and petition with thanksgiving present your requests to God and the peace of God which transcends all understanding will guard your hearts and your minds in Christ Jesus.'* (Philippians 4:6–7)

Stories of God's amazing provision could be repeated by many of us. We need to pray for our daily needs and keep on praying until we receive our answer. As we receive the provision of God, we are reminded fourthly, that we are the **people of God**.

4. People of God

Jesus went on to say:

> *'Forgive us our debts as we also have forgiven our debtors.'*
> (Matthew 6:12)

Each of us needs to give and receive forgiveness frequently because we all fail from time to time. Whenever we fail we become apprehensive, perplexed and sometimes we feel we would like to hide, to clothe ourselves under layers of falsity or fantasy. We want to hide the hurting, cringing creature within. We bank up grudges, resentments, bitterness and unforgiveness.

But Jesus said we can only expect forgiveness for our failures if we forgive those who have failed us. He said,

> *'If you forgive men when they sin against you your heavenly father will also forgive you but if you do not forgive men their sins your father will not forgive your sins.'*
> (Matthew 6:14–16)

Jesus also said,

> *'If you hold anything against anyone, forgive him so that your father in heaven may forgive you your sins.'* (Mark 11:25)

Paul later added,

> *'Bear with each other and forgive whatever grievances you may have against each other. Forgive as the Lord forgave you.'*   (Colossians 3:13)

The message is clear. Forgive and go free. If we don't forgive then we remain bound and we become spiritually, emotionally and physically sick. In fact, recently some scientists have suggested a link between unforgiveness, repressed anger and the development of some forms of cancer.

If someone has wronged us then we hold power over them because they can't do anything worse to us than they have already tried to do.

Over them we hold the power of forgiveness. It is a frightening power. If we do not forgive we will be badly hurt ourselves.

If we do forgive we release them and ourselves. Not only does Jesus urge us to forgive, he says that we ought to bless those who might so abuse us (Matthew 5:44). Therefore daily if we want to have good relationships with all of God's people we need to be praying,

> 'Father, I forgive those who have wronged and hurt me. I thank you Lord that I am also forgiven. Jesus take away those feelings of guilt, pain, failure, fear or despair that I have.'

The Apostle Paul encourages us to *'be kind to one another, tender hearted, forgiving one another, just as God in Christ forgave you'* (Ephesians 4:32).

Then fifthly, when we start to forgive as the people of God we discover the **power of God**.

5. Power of God

Jesus said:

> *'Lead us not into temptation but deliver us from the evil one.'*   (Matthew 6:13)

Here we are touching a familiar theme of spiritual warfare. We all have areas of vulnerability. We can never be complacent regarding the completeness of our own strength. When we pray, *'Lead us not into temptation, but deliver us from the evil one,'* we are affirming that our heavenly father is our deliverer and our protector. We are affirming that through Jesus we have adequate power to overcome evil (Luke 10:19).

We need to pray a hedge of protection about ourselves. Psalm 91:9–11 assures us,

> *'If you make the most high your dwelling –*
> *even the Lord who is my refuge –*
> *then no harm will befall you,*
> *no disaster will come near your tent.*
> *For he will command his angels concerning you*
> *to guard you in all your ways.'*

Satan himself reminded God that he was unable to touch Job because God had put a hedge around him, his household and everything he had (Job 1:9–11).

A Christian Armenian merchant was carrying goods by camel across the desert to a town in Turkey. Unknown to him a group of bandits were following his caravan waiting an opportunity to rob him when he camped for the night. When darkness fell they drew near. All was quiet. But to their astonishment there were no guards and they found high walls around the merchant's camp where there had been no walls before. They withdrew. Throughout the next day they followed from a distance. When night fell, again they approached only to encounter that same impassable wall.

On the third night the walls were still there but there were holes in them through which they could pass. The chief of the robber band, somewhat mystified by what had happened woke the merchant and asked him what all this meant.

The robber chief said,

> 'Ever since you left Ezerem we have been following you intending to rob you. But on the first and second nights there were high walls around your camp and so we

failed. But tonight we entered through the broken places. If you will tell us the secret of this we will molest you no further.'

The Christian merchant himself was somewhat puzzled but said,

'My friends, I have done nothing to have walls raised about us. All I do is pray every evening, committing myself and those with me to God. I fully trust in him to keep me from all evil. But tonight being very tired and sleepy, I made a rather half-hearted lip prayer. That must be why you were allowed to break in.'

Overcome by such a testimony those bandits gave themselves to Jesus Christ and from caravan robbers they became God-fearing men. But that Armenian merchant never forgot that breach in the wall of his prayer.[3]

The presence of God, the priorities of God, the provision of God, the people of God, the power for God leads us finally to the **praise of God**.

6. Praise of God

Our Lord's prayer concludes:

'*For yours is the kingdom and the glory for ever.*'

(Matthew 6:13b)

True prayer begins and ends in triumphant praise of God. Prayer is as incomplete without praise as life is without breath. We do not come into his presence to give God our advice or to praise ourselves or to seek promotion.

One mother who heard her son's demanding prayers advised him, 'Son, don't bother to give God instructions. Just report for duty!'

The Psalmist said,

'*Not to us, O Lord, not to us*
but to your name be the glory,
because of your love and faithfulness.'   (Psalm 115:1)

Unto God is the kingdom and the power and the glory because he is delivering us from every evil work. He is preserving us for his heavenly kingdom (2 Timothy 4:18; Luke 12:32). He has given us authority to overcome the works of the enemy (Luke 10:19). We are being transformed by God into the image of Jesus from glory to glory (2 Corinthians 3:18). We are participants in his kingdom.

He is the one who invites us into his presence, who sets priorities for our lives, who provides, protects and empowers us.

Therefore we shall say,

> *'For yours is the kingdom and the power and the glory for ever and ever. Amen.'*

Endnotes

1. Bilquis Sheikh, *I Dared to Call Him Father*. Eastbourne: Kingsway Publications, 1978, 38–42.
2. C.M. Ward, 'Revival Time Pulpit', *Sermon Book No. 4*, Springfield, Missouri: Assemblies of God National Radio Department, 1960, 77–79.
3. Gordon Lindsay, *Prayer That Moves Mountains*. Dallas: Christ for the Nations Inc., reprint 1984, 47–48.

Chapter 4

Hearing God

(Lamentations 3:22–26)

You know it's not going to be a good day if you happen to wake up and find that braces on your teeth have somehow locked together. The day could get even worse as you go to the bathroom to see how they can be unlocked, only to find when putting in contact lenses that you've put both lenses in the same eye.

But even worse still, one is absolutely sure it's not going to be a good day, if when driving to the dentist to solve the problem, suddenly the car horn is jammed and you realise that you're driving behind a swarm of Hell's Angels motor cyclists.

As a preacher I knew it was not going to be a good week for me when my wife walked out on my own preaching. She was ill.

By the next day she was sicker still, and I learned of a well known preacher, an acquaintance, who had suddenly died.

By Tuesday my wife was even more ill and I learned that another friend who had studied at the same theological college I had, and who had also worked overseas as a missionary, had, on a bus ride with his wife, put his head on her shoulder and gone to sleep – permanently!

On Wednesday I learned that a colleague who was placed

as a missionary in the Middle East had just been told to leave the country immediately with little notice and no reasons given. And my wife was sicker.

On Thursday I received news of yet another fine Christian woman who had been killed in a car crash. An additional personal crisis came to a head within our own family. My son-in-law was now also unwell, so I had to run his mother to the international airport at 3 am on Friday morning. Wife still sick.

As I drove back from the airport toward the city in the pre-dawn hours, I thought it was time to sit still to try to hear God. I went to one of the two cathedrals in the central business district, only to find that because of vandalism, all was now locked up and no longer accessible to the public other than in specific hours, and certainly not this early in the morning.

I thought I would go for an early pre-dawn breakfast and went to all the normal haunts of the city to find they were all closed. Finally, at about 6 am I returned to my office where I knew at least I could make a cup of coffee.

The indignity to end all, happened on Friday when I went to the local pharmacist to get antibiotics for my wife only to be asked by the lovely lady behind the counter if I had an (aged) Pension card! I guess I looked so ghastly that I was in need of an old-aged pension.

I thought how good it would have been to be able to talk to someone during the week about the many things that seemed to be 'Job-like' befalling me. But everyone seemed so busy, so preoccupied with hardly any time to listen. I couldn't help wondering whether this was the way God sometimes viewed us; so busy that we could not listen to him.

In my library I have about 50 books that deal with the subject of prayer. Only one of them has anything significant to say on the matter of hearing God. Yet, what is the point of praying to God unless we are able to hear something back from him. It is important that we learn not just to speak to God but to hear from him.

God says:

> *'Call to me and I will answer you and tell you great and unsearchable things you do not know.'*   (Jeremiah 33:3)

He is a God who listens and answers. We are a people who speak but who often don't listen for an answer. Sometimes as I watch many of the commentators on the events of daily news around the world, I wonder if anyone is listening to all of these talking heads. We all love to talk more than we love to listen. We take the same habits into our prayer life.

When we are praying alone or in the company of others, isn't it so that mostly we spend time speaking rather than listening? Yet unless we learn to listen, then our prayer is only a one-way thing which will leave us frustrated and sometimes confused.

Mother Teresa once said:

> 'I always begin my prayer in silence. It is in silence that God speaks. We need to listen because it's not what we say but what he says to and through us that matters.' [1]

King Solomon said:

> *'Do not be quick with your mouth. Do not be hasty in your heart to utter anything before God. God is in heaven and you are on earth, so let your words be few.'*   (Ecclesiastes 5:2)

Our words need to be few because of the awesomeness of the one in whose presence we stand. They also need to be few so that we might hear what God in turn has to say to us.

An ancient American Indian proverb says:

> 'Listen or your tongue will keep you deaf.'

If we think we are not receiving answers to our prayers it might be because we have not learned to listen. So often in our churches and in our prayer meetings for each person who exclaims, 'Speak (Lord), for your servant hears,' there are probably ten others who are practising, 'Listen, Lord, for your servant is speaking.'

Let's therefore look at a few things which may help us hear God.

1. Believe

We must firstly believe that God speaks. In the Bible there is the record of God speaking to Adam (Genesis 2). Again we find God speaking to Noah giving him very specific instructions (Genesis 6). God speaks to Abram (Genesis 12) and Moses (Exodus 3).

Later on there is the record of God speaking to Samuel (1 Samuel 3:2–10). He speaks to Isaiah (Isaiah 6:8–9) and to Jeremiah (Jeremiah 1:4–5, 7–8). This of course, is the way we got our Bible; God speaking to and through people.

Jesus said:

'By myself I can do nothing; I judge only as I hear.'
(John 5:30)

In other words he was listening to the Father.

Elsewhere Jesus said:

'My sheep listen to my voice.'   (John 10:16)

In Acts 8 God speaks to Phillip.
In Acts 9 he speaks to Ananias.
In Acts 10 he speaks to Peter and Cornelius.
In Acts 16 he speaks to Paul. So the record rolls on. He speaks by his Spirit.

Jesus said:

'... when he, the Spirit of truth, comes he will guide you into all truth. He will not speak on his own; he will speak only what he hears, and he will tell you what is yet to come. He will bring glory to me by taking from what is mine and making it known to you.'   (John 16:13–14)

If we are to hear God speak then we need to believe that not only did he speak in Bible times long ago, but we also need to believe that God didn't suddenly go silent when the

Bible was completed. We need to believe that according to the promise given through Jesus by the Holy Spirit, God still actually speaks and makes things known to us today. Therefore, we need to expect to hear something from him.

2. Expect to Hear

It's no use believing something but expecting nothing. George Mueller who lived in England last century was certainly a man who knew how to pray and who believed that God would speak. Mueller also expected something to happen when he prayed. He said that God had not only led him to look after 500 orphans in various homes, but that God had also provided the millions and millions of pounds that were necessary to meet the needs for that ministry. He said it all happened in response to believing, expectant prayer.

On one occasion when Mueller was travelling to Canada for a speaking engagement, dense fog had settled upon the ocean and the vessel in which he was travelling floated motionless on a silent sea. So Mr Mueller knocked anxiously on the Captain's door and said, 'I must be in Toronto by Sunday.' But the Captain replied, 'In no way can this vessel move without assuming great danger of colliding with another.'

'I understand,' said Mr Mueller. 'But in 40 years of Christian service I have not failed to keep an appointment. I must be in Toronto by Sunday.'

Then he asked the Captain to join him in special prayer so that the fog would lift. Embarrassed the Captain agreed.

They knelt and Mueller calmly asked God to lift that hindering fog. Somewhat intimidated the Captain then started to pray in order to please his anxious passenger. But no sooner had he begun when Mueller stopped him. He gently touched the Captain's shoulder saying, 'You need not pray because you do not believe.'

As the Captain and Mueller walked out onto the deck a look of sheer astonishment spread over the Captain's face.

The fog had completely lifted. George Mueller silently stood by with a look which said, 'Just as I expected it would be.'[2]

Believe that God speaks. Expect to hear and see his response. Then start to listen to him.

3. Listen

How do we listen to him?

Firstly we listen by being still. God says,

> *'Be still and know that I am God.'*   (Psalm 46:10)

If ever one tries to talk to a child when others are fidgeting or racing around, it's almost impossible to get through to have oneself heard and understood.

Similarly, God can not get through to us unless we are firstly mentally, physically, emotionally and spiritually still. One of the ways we might become still is by sitting down or kneeling or singing a quiet worship song. If distracting thoughts start to come, things which we may have forgotten to do, they can be written down on a piece of paper and put them aside till later.

If thoughts of guilt or unworthiness come to mind, we need to repent, confess and have done with them. Then we fix our attention upon Jesus.

> *'Let us fix our eyes on Jesus, the author and perfecter of our faith . . .'*   (Hebrews 12:2)

When we are still then we need to be silent. The prophet Jeremiah said:

> *'The Lord is good to those whose hope is in him, to the one who seeks him. It is good to wait quietly for the salvation of the Lord . . . Let him sit alone in silence.'*
>
>   (Lamentations 3:25–28)

We seek God by waiting in stillness before him and by remaining silent. It's interesting to speculate on why God chose Moses to be the leader of his people. Aaron was a more eloquent preacher. Korah was a more natural leader. But

Moses was chosen perhaps because in the 40 years he spent in the desert he had learnt to be still, to be silent and to listen. Similarly, Paul was required to spend three years alone in Arabia, quietly learning to listen to God.

Sometimes we think that noise is eloquence or that loudness and volume is equated with power. But that is not necessarily so. God came to Elijah as a gentle whisper (1 Kings 19:12).

Some years ago a shipping company was seeking a wireless operator. Interested applicants were notified to report for a job interview on a specific day. Many people arrived at the stated time and soon the waiting room was alive with conversation. So involved were they in their talk with one another, that among them all only one person heard a series of soft dots and dashes coming over a loud speaker hanging in the corner of the waiting room. Suddenly that man jumped to his feet and ran through the office doorway.

Later he walked from the office with a big smile because he had been given the job. The others were very surprised and even complained that they had arrived before this man and hadn't even been interviewed.[3]

But what had happened was that the owner of the shipping company had softly sent out a message in morse code over the loud speaker system saying that the first man who reported to a particular office would be offered the job. Only one man was hired because he was the only one listening. It is only as we listen that we will hear and learn.

So, believe, expect and listen.

But what are some of the ways in which God commonly speaks? Let's look at five common 'hearing aids' we need to remember.

4. Hearing Aids

(a) The Bible

The first aid he gives us is the Bible. This is still his primary method. He has gone to all the trouble of having it written down for us. We dare not overlook it.

King David said:

> *'Your word is a lamp to my feet*
> *and a light for my path.'*   (Psalm 119:105)

When we are in the dark nothing is more valuable than to have a lamp which gives light. It does not show us too far ahead or what's around the next bend in the road. Nor does it show what's beyond the corner of the building. But any lamp will show us what is immediately in front of us for the next footstep or two. And that's all we need to know.

As we meditate on the word of God, we often find that suddenly the Holy Spirit will highlight a verse or a passage and bring it to our attention and we know that God is speaking. Pastor Larry Lea once said,

> 'I'd rather fast one meal a day and spend that time reading my Bible than eat two or three meals a day and neglect the word of God. That's how important the word of God is to me.'[4]

(b) Spontaneous impressions

A second way God speaks is through spontaneous impressions.

> '...*You teach me wisdom in the inmost place.'*
>   (Psalm 51:6)

Another way of saying that is, 'in the hidden part you shall make me to know wisdom.'

In the Hebrew language the word for 'intercession' is *'paga'*. It means a 'chance encounter', or an 'accidental intersecting'. If we are sensitive enough, God will develop our capacity to hear through spontaneous impressions brought about by the Holy Spirit. This is why we must develop a personal relationship with the Holy Spirit. Furthermore, we only become aware of his nature as we enter into a life of prayer.

Pastor David Yonggi Cho of Korea has written of his own 'life changing discovery'. One day the Lord said to him, 'You must get to know and work with the Holy Spirit.'

'"Up to that time," Pastor Cho says, "I had always thought of the Holy Spirit as an experience and not as a personality. I realised that getting to know the Holy Spirit would require my spending time talking with him and letting him talk to me. The key to hearing from God and obtaining direction is through fellowship with the Holy Spirit."'[5]

Rees Howells of England was a great man of prayer. Once when he was departing for Africa he got ready to board a train for London where he would board a ship. But he found that between him and his companion they had only ten shillings. That was only enough to take them about 20 miles on the train. Rees Howells later wrote about what happened:

'We felt sure the money would come so we went to the platform to wait for it to arrive. The time for the train to depart came so we decided to go as far as possible. Leaving the train 20 miles later we met some friends who invited us for breakfast. Surely God had sent these friends to pay the way, we thought. But the departure time arrived and no offers of financial help were given. Then the Holy Spirit spoke to me and said, "If you had money what would you do?" I replied, "I would take my place in the line at the ticket counter."

"Well, are you not preaching that my promises are equal to the need?" replied the Spirit. "You had better take your place in the line."

So we stood in the line as if we had money for the ticket. When there were only two people before me a man stepped out of the crowd and said, "I am sorry. I can't wait any longer. I must open my shop." He said goodbye and put 30 shillings into my hand.'[6]

Rees Howells had learned to recognise God's voice through the spontaneous impressions that came to him through the Holy Spirit.

(c) Dreams and Visions

A third way in which God speaks is through dreams and visions. Dreams are that which may occur while we sleep. Visions are that which may be 'seen' while we are awake.

To the prophet Joel God said:

> *'Afterward I will pour out my Spirit on all people. Your sons and daughters will prophesy. Your old men will dream dreams. Your young men will see visions.'* (Joel 2:38)

That prophecy started to be fulfilled in the book of Acts. Peter referred to it (Acts 2:17). Dreams and visions have always been one of the commonest ways in which God has spoken to people. That was the way in which he spoke to Joseph (Genesis 37) and to Daniel. The Bible says:

> *'In the first year of Belshazzar, King of Babylon, Daniel had a dream and visions passed through his mind as he was lying on his bed. He wrote down the substance of his dream.'*
> (Daniel 7:1)

In Asia where I worked for 14 years, many of the people who came to accept Jesus Christ did so because firstly God had spoken to them in dreams. That is a common experience in many other less developed countries. It is only in the developed western countries that people have become so rational and seemingly sophisticated as to try to bypass one of the obvious ways outlined in the Bible in which God speaks. One of the ways God spoke to me concerning my call from ministry in Asia to work in Australia, was through a very specific dream.

We need to reconsider and expect that God will continue to speak through dreams and visions.

(d) Release and Peace

A fourth way in which God speaks is that we will experience a sudden release accompanied by peace. We will 'know' within our spirit that God is speaking. Again an illustration from the life of Rees Howells is so apt.

In September 1943 a critical battle was being fought in World War II. The Allies were trying to establish a beachhead in Salerno in Italy against the Axis powers. If they could succeed they would then be able to march on Rome. Back in England Rees Howells was leading a prayer meeting. The record of that prayer meeting is as follows:

> 'We had the first evening prayer meeting as usual in the Conference Hall and gathered again at 9.45 pm. The meeting had a solemn tone from the outset. The director, Mr Howells, whose voice was trembling with the burden of his message and was scarcely audible said, "The Lord has burdened me with the invasion of Salerno. I believe our men are in great danger of losing their hold." He then called the congregation to prayer. It was not an ordinary prayer time. Prayer was intense and urgent and in the greatest sense, true prevailing prayer.
>
> The Spirit took hold of us and suddenly broke right through. We found ourselves praising and rejoicing, believing that God had heard and answered. We could not go on praying any longer so we arose, the Spirit witnessing in all our hearts that God had wrought some miraculous intervention in Italy. The victory was so outstanding that we looked at the clock as we rose to sing. It was the stroke of 11 pm.'

Rees Howells claimed that he had heard God and started to pray until there came a great release and peace. Did he hear correctly? Here's what happened as recorded elsewhere in history.

A few days later a war correspondent filed an account of the Salerno battle using the headline, 'The Miracle of Salerno'.

He was with the troops in Salerno and he said:

> 'The enemy was advancing rapidly and increasing devastation was evident. It was obvious that unless a miracle happened, the city would be lost. British troops had insufficient strength to stop the advance until the

beachhead was established. Suddenly without reason, firing ceased and deathlike stillness settled. We waited in breathless anticipation but nothing happened. I looked at my watch and it was 11 pm. Still we waited, but still nothing happened. Nothing happened all night. But those hours made all the difference to the invasion. By morning the beachhead was established.'[7]

Rees Howells acted on the spontaneous impression that God wanted them to pray. They kept on praying until there was release and peace, until they 'knew' that God had spoken and acted. Joy and peace returned. Isn't that precisely what the Apostle Paul said it should be like?

> 'Do not be anxious about anything, but in everything by prayer and petition with thanksgiving, present your requests to God and the peace of God (there's that sudden release) which transcends all understanding (in other words don't try to analyse it just accept it) will guard your hearts and your minds in Christ Jesus.' (Philippians 4:6–7)

(e) Through Others

A fifth way in which God often speaks is through others. The Bible says:

> 'Plans fail for lack of counsel but with many advisers they succeed.' (Proverbs 15:22)

As we listen to other godly advisers, God so often speaks confirming words through them.

I was called into ministry through one of the leaders of my home church. I was called into missionary work in Asia through a fellow student at theological college. I was even told who my wife was to be by another of the leaders of my home church.

I never make a major decision alone. I always carefully check it out with the other members of my pastoral team and members of our church council. These are people of maturity who know how to wait on God and to listen to him to confirm or otherwise what may be of God for us.

God gives us at least five hearing aids: the Bible, spontaneous impressions, dreams or visions, release and peace, other believers.

To improve our hearing ability further, fifthly, we should write down what we think God is saying.

5. Response

(a) Write Down

God said to the prophet Habakkuk:

> *'Write down the revelation and make it plain on tablets.'*
> (Habakkuk 2:2)

For us the modern equivalent would be to keep a notebook of the things that we think God might be saying to us. As we go back through our diaries or journals we might be surprised to discover the trends of how God has been directing our lives. If we don't keep a note of it, we may forget it and that could be to our own loss.

(b) Obey

Finally, whatever God says – do it! Obedience is always a major key. Abraham was such a great man in God to the point where he became called a 'friend of God'. This was because he always obeyed. Jesus likewise calls us friends. But there is a condition to that friendship.

Jesus said:

> *'If you love me, you will obey what I command.'*
> (John 14:15)

David Yonggi Cho of Korea was once asked how he was used to build such a great church of three quarters of a million members. His reply was simple, 'I pray and I obey!'[8]

Lot's of people want to obey but they do not pray. Some people pray but don't have the courage to obey.

American preacher Kathryn Kuhlman once said, 'If you're

going to be led by the Holy Spirit you have to be willing to follow.'

God is unlikely to speak to us if he knows that we have no intention of doing what he asks of us.

Through Jeremiah God says:

> *'Call to me and I will answer you and tell you great and unsearchable things you do not know.'*   (Jeremiah 33:3)

May it be so as we:

- believe
- expect
- listen – using our five hearing aids
- write down what he says and
- are prepared to obey him.

Endnotes

1.   Subin Bhaumik, Meenakshi Ganguly, Tim McGirk. 'Seeker of Souls', *Time*, September 15 1997, 73.
2.   Dick Eastman, *No Easy Road*. Grand Rapids, Michigan: Baker Book House, 1971, 19.
3.   Dick Eastman, *Change the World School of Prayer*. Penshurst, Australia: World Literature Crusade, 1983, C-75, 76.
4.   Larry Lea, *The Hearing Ear*. Altamonte Springs, Florida: Creation House, 1988, 75.
5.   Paul Y. Cho, *Prayer: Key to Revival*. Waco, Texas: Word Publishing, 1985, 38.
6.   Dick Eastman, *No Easy Road*. Grand Rapids, Michigan: Baker Book House, 1971, 21, 22.
7.   *Ibid*, 101, 102.
8.   Larry Lea, *Could You Not Tarry One Hour*. Altamonte Springs, Florida: Creation House, 1987, 47.

Chapter 5

Checking It Out
(Matthew 17:1–5)

A railway conductor began checking tickets on a morning train and discovered that the first passenger he checked out had the wrong ticket.

'I'm sorry sir,' said the conductor, 'but you're on the wrong train. You'll have to change at the next station.'

As he moved through the carriage checking tickets at random he found that there were other passengers who were also carrying the wrong tickets. It seemed strange to him that so many people should have made the same mistake. Then it suddenly dawned on him. It was not they but he who was on the wrong train! [1]

How many times in life do we find ourselves following a particular course of action, absolutely convinced that we have heard from God correctly, only to find that we were to varying degrees quite mistaken.

If 'the ultimate end and the supreme motive for each Christian is the will of God,' [2] the problem becomes, how do we know we've found it? Sure we pray. But prayer is usually our talking. We're not good at listening.

God himself said:

> 'This is my son, whom I love; with him I am well pleased. Listen to him!'
> (Matthew 17:5)

If prayer is giving at least equal time to listening to God, how can we become more confident that we are in fact hearing correctly, especially on the major issues of life? And how can we more validly cross-check those often self-appointed counsellors who somewhat readily want to speak into our lives 'in the name of the Lord'?

To increase confidence that we are in fact hearing God correctly I offer a few recommendations. Take the best and leave the rest.

1. Stop

The apostle Paul encouraged early Roman believers to understand that if they wanted to know what God's will was and to be able presumably to hear him more clearly, then a prerequisite for that was that they should offer their own bodies as living sacrifices. This certainly pleases God (Romans 12:1–2). In short, we have to stop wanting our own will.

The most difficult part of any process is often the beginning. The journey of more accurately hearing God in prayer is not dissimilar.

Dying to self is the most difficult step. People around the world and especially in the self-indulgent western world find it difficult to die to self. In saying that we are to be living sacrifices Paul was speaking against a background in which animal sacrifice was clearly understood. Still today in many countries of other religious persuasions animals are regularly sacrificed.

It is a common scene at certain times within the various religious calendars that hundreds of thousands of animals will be purchased, preened and taken to appropriate places to be sacrificed. The animals are carefully trussed up. It is then attempted, mostly, to lay them down on the ground, after which their throats are cut and the blood drained out.

Having watched this process countless times I have often noticed that occasionally an animal will intuitively understand that what is about to happen is hardly in its best interest. It will struggle and sometimes break free and flee. At that point of course it fails to fulfil the fundamental condition for which it was appointed – to be a sacrifice.

The moment we exercise self-will we also fail to be in a position where we can hear God clearly. We are, as it were, to lay down as living sacrifices. Ultimately through listening prayer we may also come to understand what is God's 'good, pleasing and perfect will' on various matters affecting our lives. There is no other way to commence to discover what God might significantly want to say to us other than by giving up on our own will. Having done that we need to look into his word.

2. Look

In cross-checking whether we have heard from God we should never overlook his already clearly revealed word to us as it exists in his written book – the Bible.

Psalm 119:105 says:

> 'Your word is a lamp to my feet
> and a light to my path.'

In the same Psalm it says that:

> 'The entrance of your words gives light;
> it gives understanding to the simple.'   (Psalm 119:130)

Because many of us live in the developed, industrialised world we fail to realise the force of the word of God being a lamp and a light. In the age in which these words were written and still today in many countries, no one would walk out into the darkness without some sort of light and also preferably a stick.

Unlike the carefully manicured, paved, well-lit footpaths on which many walk in the cities of the world, still today in most of the world's less developed countries, to go out at night without light and a stick is crazy. People may fall down holes, or step on a snake or slip on animal or human excrement. There are all sorts of literal pitfalls for the person who walks in darkness.

Often a kerosene or similarly lit lantern is carried. It shows enough of the way forward just to see what lies ahead for the next couple of steps. It does not show anything in the far distance nor does it show what may be around the next corner. But we don't need to know that. We need to know only what is the next step.

Revelation of what God wants to say to us comes through the written word in two ways.

Firstly, there is the general revelation of that which is throughout the Bible. There will be principles by which we are meant to live. There will be slabs of Scripture which pertain to specific situations in life.

Shortly after I became a follower of Jesus, intuitively I stopped having a different girlfriend every month. They all looked rather wonderful to me but I knew that I needed somehow to find God's choice.

With new-found childish faith, I prayed every night that God would lead me to the woman of his choice. And then after religiously concluding with ... 'In Jesus' name Amen', when I thought I couldn't be heard, I'd add, 'Let her be like Marilyn Monroe!'

My problem was that I was ignorant of much of which was written in the word of God. Had I been aware of the teaching in Proverbs 31 of the qualities of a godly woman, that probably would have knocked out about 99.5% of the women I knew as prospective candidates.

We often wonder why God seems silent. In fact he is not silent. He has already clearly spoken and he expects us to search out the answers recorded in black and white in his word. Why should he speak twice specifically for any of us when he has taken all the trouble to have everything so well recorded and documented.

The second form of revelation occurs when we are reading through the Scriptures and suddenly the Holy Spirit will, as it were, hit us between the eyes with a verse or a passage in a way which we may never have noticed or applied ever before. This is known as a *'rhema'*. It's a particular revelation that the

Spirit wants to give us at that time to meet a specific situation.

Either way, we must be diligent in searching constantly in the word of God where so much that we need to know is already revealed for us. We also need to keep in mind that God is never going to speak contrary to his word. That will become clear as we also listen to godly counsel.

3. Listen

The book of Proverbs strongly advises seeking out good counsel (Proverbs 11:14; 12:15; 15:22 and 20:18). In an age when (western) Christianity has been individualised and privatised, we forget that we are a part of the community of God and are meant to draw upon wisdom which he has placed within that community for our benefit.

Each person knows some other believer whom they respect in God, who may or may not hold office within a local church community. It may be a pastor, a deacon, an elder or it may just be a godly relative or mature friend. Whoever it is, we are well advised to check out with more mature people who know us well as to the accuracy of whether or not we are hearing appropriately from God. Unless it is confirmed by some such, then it may be that what we think we hear is little more than that which arises from our own desires or emotions.

Stopping, looking and listening are the first three basic steps in the process of hearing God more accurately.

In primary school many of us learned a jingle to help us remember some basic road safety procedures. 'Stop, look and listen before you cross the road . . . ' If we don't do that we may end up splattered underneath some speeding vehicle.

In life in general, we may similarly be splattered, broken or hurt if before we act, we fail to stop, look and listen to God which is precisely what happened to Kings Jehosophat and Ahab (2 Chronicles 18). But having done that we are at least ready to test the situation.

4. Test

The test of circumstance is often a great hearing aid but is always open to abuse. We have an innate tendency to interpret the significance of circumstance in terms of our own desires.

If the prophet Jonah had walked into some of our churches today without our knowing the background of what God had told him to do, he could have fooled many by giving a fantastic testimony all based on circumstance.

He could have spun a story about how he just happened to be walking along the wharves and he just happened to find a sea-captain who just happened to have a ship on which there just happened to be one remaining empty berth and he just happened to have the right amount of money to pay for his ticket and it all happened sequentially so perfectly it could only be God! It would sound so plausible and persuasive a story that we would buy into it and confirm it with a 'Praise the Lord', if we didn't know that instead of sailing south-west, God had told Jonah to walk north-east to Nineveh.

Some years ago I was approached by a Christian woman advising me of a course of action which she wanted to take which would lead her to divorce her own husband and marry another Christian, all three of whom were members of the same church. She spoke so persuasively as to the alleged guidance God had given. Circumstantially there could be quite a case if one disregarded the word of God and the degree to which passion had prejudiced the interpretation and outcome of God's previously written clear directions.

The problem with circumstances is not only do we mis-interpret to benefit our own comfort, but they can be deceiving. In Joshua 9 we read how the Gibeonites dressed themselves as if they were ambassadors from a different nation. In fact they were immediate neighbours to the newly promised land. But their disguise was so effective as to fool the Israelites who did not seek the counsel of God but allowed themselves to be persuaded solely by circumstance (Joshua 9:14).[3]

The concept of Gideon's fleece (Judges 6) is helpful but it is never the final arbiter in cross-checking the accuracy with which we think we may be hearing God.

5. Trust

No matter how many checks we put in place, ultimately we are required to walk by faith (Habakkuk 2:4; Romans 1:17; Hebrews 11:1). It is only as we step out in faith that we are going to prove whether or not through prayer we have accurately heard God. There are plenty of people who boast that they hear God clearly, but then carefully manipulate circumstances so as never to be obliged actually to put their discernment to the test.

When I worked in South Asia I often came to river crossings where 'the bridge' was only a few bamboo poles lashed together. Somehow I had to cross with my motor cycle. The normal process was to shuffle slowly backwards pulling the motor cycle behind one. The question always was, would the bamboo support such weight? If it was new, green and fresh the prospect of safe passage was a reasonable risk. But if the bamboo had dried out and become brittle then the probability of crashing into the water was greatly increased.

On such occasions I would always ask those boatmen nearest the crossing about the state of the bamboo. Usually they would encourage me to have a go. Not satisfied by their word, for they would after all gain revenue if they had to fish me out from the water, I would ask nearby shopkeepers for their opinions. They also usually answered in the affirmative, because should I fall in the water they could then sell me cups of hot tea. I could have made enquiries up to the national level at a board of road construction engineers. Regardless of advice received, I would never know whether I could trust that bridge until I actually stepped out on it with my motor cycle in tow.

It's only as we start to take specific steps of faith, that we are going to know whether or not what we claim to have heard from God, is in fact so or merely a figment of our own imagination. But the results will show very quickly.

6. Peace

One of the first indicators that the step we are taking is truly that which we have heard from God or not is whether we retain peace (Isaiah 26:3).

Peace is something which is difficult to describe because it's beyond understanding (Philippians 4:6–7). But that which the Bible says we will have, is something which we know when we've got it and we surely know when we've lost it. If in prayer we have heard accurately and are responding appropriately then that peace will be retained. If we lose it, we need to return immediately to the place where we last had it. And in all of this we are never alone. We have the Holy Spirit.

7. The Holy Spirit

In prayer, often it seems that God is silent. For whatever reason we don't seem to be able to hear him. We then imagine that we are bereft, abandoned, left alone in the universe to fend for ourselves to stumble into an uncertain future.

We need to remind ourselves that the Holy Spirit is there to help and to guide us, whether or not we are aware of his presence. (John 14:15, 26, 27; 16:7, 13, 14). Jesus made very specific promises as to the Holy Spirit's availability to us and his guidance of us.

The record in the book of Acts is one of the church praying and waiting on God for the answers brought to them by the Holy Spirit. He did then and he still does today. Just as the earliest disciples had to wait in Jerusalem for both their empowerment and their direction, so today we also may be obliged to wait.

But that requires an application of that all too scarce commodity – patience!

8. Patience

Peter reminds us that:

> *'With the Lord a day is like a thousand years, and a thousand years are like a day. The Lord is not slow in keeping his promise as some understand slowness.'* (2 Peter 3:8–9)

To this, the writer to the Hebrews adds:

> *'...do not throw away your confidence; it will be richly rewarded. You need to persevere so that when you have done the will of God, you will receive what he has promised.'*
> (Hebrews 10:35–36)

Today we live in a world of instant gratification – instant dessert, instant tea, instant coffee, instant soup, instant marriage, instant divorce, instant birth through IVF and instant death through euthanasia. We even wear watches which measure time in hundredths of a second, of which we are never likely to take any notice.

When it comes to waiting upon God in prayer we forget that he for whom 'a thousand years are like a day,' is seldom in the same hurry as our busy little minds demand of him.

In effect, what we often do is to zoom into his presence at our appointed hour with our needs list. In prayer, we wander down the aisles of our minds as if we were shopping in a supermarket, highlighting the various items we wish to note as we go. Rapidly we pass on through the check-out point of our prayer life with a panted 'Amen'. Then, as we move on into an ever busy day, we frequently add, 'And please let it be done right now.'

If God does not immediately answer, we say he has gone on holiday or he's not listening. Either way we've got no answer. So what's the point of prayer?

We forget how long it took the angel to reach Daniel with the answer to his prayer (Daniel 10:12–13). We forget that God is not required to pay his debts the way many of us are, according to the various taxation regimes and end of financial year commitments in the countries in which we live. He requires patience. Patience may not change our circumstances but it will surely change us.

For us patience which is meant to pass on to perseverance seems an unreasonable burden. So we chop our prayer life and pass on quickly to some other activity. But it seems that as we look at nature we can learn great lessons.

After fresh rainfall, streams on mountain sides could not sing if all rocks were removed from them. When we encounter a 'rock' or similar difficulty in the pathway of our life, we want it kicked aside. If we did that with mountain streams, we'd end up with little more than mud sluices.

Do we want our lives to sing and bubble like mountain streams or just to slurp like pig's swill?

In the 1980s a popularly sung song had a line by which we invited the Lord to make us ... 'like precious stones, crystal clear and finely honed'. The most precious stone is a diamond, which in simplest terms is a huge dollop of mud subjected to enormous pressure and heat. Are we serious in inviting God to speak to us through situations of intense pressure and heat?

The first time I saw vast fields of unharvested lavender flowers I enquired as to what would happen to them. I was advised that they would all be cut down and crushed. Out of so many crushed flowers there would emerge tiny drops of pure essence sufficient to perfume thousands of bottles of aftershave lotion or eau de cologne.

When bread or cakes are rising under heat in the oven, immature children want to open the oven door to see the source of such aroma. Inevitably that which is cooking in the heat is ruined.

We need to remember that as we are waiting on God in prayer for him to speak, when things get tough or hot we do not move. People and pressures shift, but the soil remains the same wherever we go.

That to which I have referred above merely indicates some of the listening and cross-checking devices we need to develop. I personally never reach a major decision unless every one of them is in place. It's like bringing a plane down to land or guiding a boat into harbour. All the lights on the starboard and port sides as well as the glide path need to be lined up accurately and precisely. If one or two of them are out of position, the danger is there will be a crash of the plane or a grounding of the boat.

When the above indicators are in place, we can be far more assured that we are hearing God more accurately.

He certainly wants to make known his ways to us even more than we might want to know them. Remember the best way to hear God's guidance is to get to know the guide (John 10:3–4).

Endnotes

1. Warren Wiersbe, *Confident Living*. Good News Broadcasting Association, Inc. 1988.
2. Harold Lindsell, *An Evangelical Theology of Missions*. Grand Rapids, Michigan: Zondervan Publishing House.
3   G.J. Glen, 'How Can I Know God's Will in My Life?' *Australia's New Day*, May 1982, 16.

Chapter 6

Hindrances

(Psalm 66:16–20)

A while ago a member of my family was struggling with a personal issue. During the course of that struggle, I heard her say something like this:

> We have prayed and prayed about this matter, but we don't seem to get anywhere. Doesn't God hear? If he is listening, why doesn't he help? Why doesn't he answer our prayers?

Many people often find themselves in that situation. They believe in God. They believe the Bible. They attend church regularly. They witness to their faith. They know that the Holy Spirit dwells within. But when things are tough and they pray fervently about something, God doesn't seem to answer. Or if he does answer, it's in a way which they cannot perceive or understand.

In that situation, they become like my motor car. There was a time when my daughter was driving our car. It was noticed that it was suddenly overheating. My wife was called in to help. She did what she could without too much success.

So here is a car. It looks good. Its motor is in excellent condition. The tyres are all pumped up to the right pressure. There is plenty of petrol in the tank and oil in the engine. There are not even any squeaks. We sit in the car ready to go and either we go nowhere or at best we move such a small distance, overheat and stop again.

When we find ourselves in that situation, and many of us do frequently, how do we respond? Do we say, 'I give up. I don't believe in motor cars. I'll walk. In fact, I don't think motor cars have ever existed!'

Of course we don't react that way. We set to work to find out where the problem lies. In the case of our car, it was a small radiator hose which had sprung a leak. Once that was fixed, the vehicle purred off once more.

If we think that we are not moving ahead in God and that our prayers are not being answered, then rather than cease believing in the existence of God, it's better if we took time to have a look to see where else the problem could be. In doing that, we may be surprised to learn that the problem was never with God, but was with us.

The Bible and many others affirm that God is alive. He hears our prayers and he wants to answer them. When they appear not to be answered, we need to go back to basics and check out the fault-finding systems of our relationships with him.

Evelyn Christenson is a pastor's wife. She decided to meet with two prayer partners weekly to pray for their church. As they came together each week, they found they could get nowhere. For six weeks the Lord directed them to Psalm 66:18 which says:

> *'If I had cherished sin in my heart,*
> *the Lord would not have listened.'*

'Us? With sin in our hearts!' thought those ladies.
'Well, the Bible does say in 1 Peter 3:12 that:

> *"The eyes of the Lord are on the righteous and his ears are attentive to their prayer, but the face of the Lord is against those who do evil."'*

'Sin in our hearts? Well, that would certainly stop God acting on our prayer,' they thought.

As they waited on God they found that they had not been practising any of the spectacular sins that we sometimes hear in public. But God did expose matters of pride, self-satisfaction, critical thoughts and pretence on their part.[1]

The prophet Isaiah said:

> *'Your iniquities have separated you from your God. Your sins have hidden his face from you so that he will not hear.'*
>
> (Isaiah 59:1–2)

So many people cry out to God while continuing to cherish unconfessed sin. And it is that sin which separates.

There are many references in the Bible that clearly state that prayer will not be answered if certain things are within us. We need to look at these areas, but not in the sense of bringing anyone under judgment. That is not our responsibility. Only God is our judge. But there is a need to develop a check chart whereby if, at this time or at some time in the future, we feel that we are not getting through to God, then we will be able to take it out, check through it and ask the Holy Spirit to reveal in which particular areas of our lives the problem might be.

As in God's sight there are no big sins and little sins, just sin, so items on this non-exhaustive list are not in any particular order of priority.

1. Unforgiveness/Criticism

The first area we need to look at is that of unforgiveness and criticism. These two are linked because it is so difficult to separate them, and they are probably the most common hindrance to answered prayer.

The writer of Hebrews said:

> *'See to it that no one misses the grace of God and that no bitter root grows up to cause trouble and defile many.'*
>
> (Hebrews 12:14–15)

Jesus said:

> *'If you do not forgive men their sins, your Father will not forgive your sins.'*
>
> (Matthew 6:14–15)

He additionally said:

> '*If you hold anything against anyone, forgive him so that your Father in heaven may forgive your sins.*' (Mark 11:25)

> *If you are offering your gift at the altar and there remember that your brother has something against you, leave your gift there in front of the altar. First go and be reconciled to your brother; then come and offer your gift.*' (Matthew 5:23–24)

If we do not have good, open, healthy relationships with everyone, then our prayer life is going to be hindered.

When we come to God in prayer, we come on the basis that our sins are forgiven in Jesus Christ. He in turn asks that we forgive all others. If we do not, he will not.

If we do not forgive, we develop a critical attitude, and that in turn leads to bitterness, resentment, animosity, coldness – even hatred. If we hold a grudge or maintain ill-will toward anyone, then God is closed off from us. If there are unresolved issues between us and another, then we may pray all we like, but those prayers may go no further than the ceiling.

Forgiveness may not be easy. But Jesus regarded it as so important that he did not ask us to forgive, he commanded it.

Many years ago there was a man called Hyde, who for a time worked as a missionary in India. He was very careful with whatever he said in public. No critical word ever left his lips. But his prayer life was slightly different.

One day as he knelt to pray, he felt a keen burden to pray for an Indian pastor. He started to talk to the Lord about this pastor's unfortunate mannerisms, of how cold he seemed to be. But then a finger seemed to touch Hyde's lips sealing them shut. Mr Hyde believed he heard the voice of God softly say to him, 'He who touches that pastor touches the apple of my eye.'

So Hyde immediately cried out, 'Father forgive me. I have been an accomplice of Satan. I have been an accuser of the brethren before you.'

Hyde begged God to show to him instead good things in this pastor's life. As they came into his mind, he prayed over those good things and started to praise God for this pastor. Shortly afterwards, revival broke out in that Indian church. One of the releases of that was that the blockage of silent criticism had been removed from Hyde's prayer life.[2]

In a world which is littered by protest signs, with our streets often clogged by demonstrators, with newspaper editors constantly seeking for something to pounce upon, and Parliamentarians throwing insults at one another, it's so easy for Christians to slip into the unforgiving, harsh, critical spirit of our age.

We need to resist that lest we inhibit what God might be really wanting to do in our lives and through his church.

A Turkish soldier had beaten a Christian prisoner until he was only half-conscious. As he continued to kick him he shouted, 'What can your Christ do for you now?' The reply? 'He can give me strength to forgive you.'[3]

2. Indiscipline

A second reason for our prayers being hindered may be indiscipline.

The great dividing line between success and failure in many things, may often be expressed in just five words: 'I did not make time.'

The reason we do not make time for particular things is usually because we do not consider them important enough. They rate low on our priorities.

The apostle Paul challenged the Roman Governor Felix to consider the claims of Christ. But Felix replied, *'That's enough for now. When I find it convenient, I will send for you'* (Acts 24:25).

The problem is, for such matters a convenient time often never comes. For the development of one's spiritual life, a full diary often leads to an empty heart.

We can spend a great deal of time working in the kingdom of God, but give little time to waiting on the King himself. The substitute for blessedness is often busyness which leads to barrenness. We become too busy to love, too busy to share, too busy to care and too busy to pray. We need to discipline ourselves to set our priorities in order.

God says:

> *'Be still and know that I am God.'*   (Psalm 46:10)

A former British journalist Malcolm Muggeridge once said that:

> 'God is the friend of silence, because he speaks only when we are quiet.'

David Watson was an English evangelist who, through his preaching, tapes and writing, exercised an internationally influential ministry. A few months after he had had an operation for cancer, just prior to his death, he said:

> 'God showed me that all my preaching, writing and other ministry was absolutely nothing compared with my love relationship with him. In fact, sheer busyness had squeezed out the close intimacy I had known with him.' [4]

Sister Briege McKenna, a lady to whom God gave a powerful healing ministry, made a commitment to spend three hours a day with God in prayer. She said:

> 'I've had to remind myself continually that I need Jesus more than people need me. If I don't go to Jesus in prayer, I would have nothing to offer them. I don't pray because I am holy, but because I want to become holy and I need Jesus to teach me.
>
> We forget sometimes that Jesus is a living person who waits for us. When we pray we are not committing time to a project, but to a living person. Jesus is there not for what I can give him, but for what he gives to me.' [5]

Charles Mahaney told of how for years he struggled to become consistent in prayer. Finally when he asked the Lord why he was unable to pray more, he got an unusual response. He says, 'I wasn't ready for the answer the Lord gave.

Expecting an insight that I had yet to hear in all my study of the subject, the reply came, "You're lazy!"'

Mahaney had trouble getting up in the morning because he was undisciplined in going to bed sufficiently early. He had to realise that God did little in his life after 10.30 pm anyway.[6]

The apostle Peter wrote that we need to be *'clear minded and self-controlled so that* (we) *can pray'* (1 Peter 4:7). He later went on to say that self-control leads to perseverance and perseverance leads to godliness (2 Peter 1:6).

Without self-control, perseverance and discipline we will never set and keep to the priorities needed to develop the relationship with God which he desires for us.

3. Idolatry

The third area we need to check out is that of idolatry. An idol is anything which takes the place of God as the supreme object of our affection. While no Christian should ever have an image in their home before which they would bow down and worship, we may certainly have other idols, maybe even the homes themselves.

What takes first priority in our lives? Is it a husband or a wife? Is it our children? Is it our reputation and social standing? Is it career advancement, financial status or security? Is it ambition or just a desire to travel extensively overseas? Is it a self-imposed demand always to have the home, garden or car absolutely spotless?

Many centuries ago God said through his prophet Ezekiel:

> *'These men have set up idols in their hearts and put wicked stumbling blocks before their faces. Should I let them enquire of me at all?'* (Ezekiel 14:3)

To which Jesus adds:

> *'Anyone who loves his father or mother . . . son or daughter . . .* (much more than me) *is not worthy of me. Anyone*

who does not take his cross and follow me is not worthy of
me.'
(Matthew 10:37–38)

If God is not absolutely first continuously in our lives, then
our relationship with him is impaired.

4. Broken Promises

The fourth area we need to touch upon, is that of broken
promises. In the Psalms we read:

'Fulfil your vows to the most high ...
I will deliver you...'
(Psalm 50:14–15)

Someone was speaking to me recently who had been
struggling in the area of God's seeming silence. This person
had been waiting on God for some answers to prayer when
God reminded her of a certain promise she'd made but
hadn't kept. Praise God! She's doing something about it and
God has once more become real to her and is giving answers
to her prayer.

5. Disobedience

The fifth area to look at is that of disobedience.
John wrote:

'We receive from (God) *anything we ask because we obey his*
commands and do what pleases him.'   (1 John 3:22–23)

Lives which consistently please God are those which
consistently obey him. Jesus said:

'If you remain in me and my words remain in you, ask
whatever you wish and it will be given you.'   (John 15:7)

As we both obey and remain in Jesus, then he moves
powerfully into our lives. If we will not, then he does not.

6. Unbelief

The sixth area to examine is unbelief.

The apostle James was spot on when he said:

> '...when anyone asks (of God) he must believe and not doubt, because he who doubts is like a wave of the sea, blown and tossed by the wind. That man should not think he will receive anything form the Lord; he is a double minded man, unstable in all he does.'
> (James 1:6–8)

One of the greatest inhibitors to God answering our prayers, is that we do not really believe what we are saying. This attitude leads to spiritual power failures. Because we have difficulty in belief, we tend in our prayer life to retreat into vague generalities. We do this because we don't want to put God to the test, because we don't think he can meet the test. In essence in faith, we ask for nothing – so that's exactly what we receive – nothing.

We content ourselves with vague prayers about peace on earth. But we do not pray for peace within our own families.

We pray that the Lord will provide for the poor of the world. But we will not pray that he help us find the money to pay the electricity bill next week.

We ask him to bless missionaries in far off places, or to convert the heathen, but we never ask for too much specifically regarding our own lives, or that he should convert someone within our own household.

We treat prayer like window shopping – which can be an enjoyable way to pass the time. It costs nothing and it results in nothing. We do this because we doubt God's ability to measure up to his seemingly impossible promises. Or perhaps we are not too specific because we are afraid that his answer will be 'no' and that would mean our having to give up something onto which we'd rather hang.

When we come to God, we need to remember that we are not just coming to our king, but also to our heavenly Father who is vitally concerned about the big and the little things of our lives. The gospel of Mark records the story of the man with the demon-possessed son whom no one else was able to help (Mark 9:14–32). With that terrible affliction the father came to Jesus. In his distress he said:

> ' *"If you can do anything, take pity on us and help us.'*
> *To which Jesus replied, "If I can? Everything is possible for him who believes."*
> *The father then said, "I do believe. Help me overcome my unbelief."* '

If we have trouble with unbelief, then we need to confess that also to our heavenly Father. We need to tell him of our feelings of helplessness and failure, and ask him to help us overcome our unbelief. Remember, God is personal. He is listening. He will reply and act if we wait and permit him.

7. Wilfulness

The seventh area we need to check out is that of wilfulness. God may not seem to be answering our prayers because we decline firstly to submit ourselves to discern his will. The Bible says:

> *'When you ask, you do not receive, because you ask with wrong motives . . . '*
> (James 4:3)

It also says:

> *'If we ask anything according to God's will, he hears us.'*
> (1 John 5:14)

What often happens, is that our prayers are self-motivated. We want them to be answered because it will bring self-fulfilment, self-satisfaction, or the praise of others. We drift into a situation where we are trying to build our own kingdom rather than God's kingdom. We want our desires gratified. We want to be vindicated. We might even be hoping for revenge. God does not deal with us on the basis of any such motives. It is only as we come as Jesus did praying, *'Not my will but your will be done,'* (Mark 14:36) that he will show us what he requires.

81

A woman who went to a prayer seminar testified as follows:

'My initial reaction to the prayer seminar was "What good will it do?" I have prayed and prayed and it hasn't done any good. I have been a Christian all my life. Now my husband's construction company has folded, leaving enormous debts. We have had to sell our home, liquidate our assets and also our young son has just undergone surgery. For some time I have been praying for what I wanted to happen. Suddenly, I saw something new. I had not prayed for God's will to be done. So I said aloud, "Lord, I want your perfect will for me and my family." That was it. I was to learn later that what was keeping my prayers from being answered was that I had never asked God for his will.

Now I am free. The whole load is lifted. The responsibility to straighten out this mess is no longer mine and at last I know peace. My husband's debts are being paid. My health has improved. I was offered a job when I wasn't even searching for one. This new train of events started once I totally surrendered my will in every matter to the will of God.'[7]

'Not my will, Father, but yours be done' is often the opening prayer to seeing God answer and act in ways in our lives.

Therefore let us humbly come before him again, but keeping in mind the words of Isaiah 55:8–9 where God says:

'...*My thoughts are not your thoughts,*
neither are your ways my ways ...
As the heavens are higher than the earth,
so are my ways higher than your ways,
and my thoughts than your thoughts.'

'*Let us then approach the throne of grace with confidence, so that we may receive mercy and find grace to help us in our time of need.'*
(Hebrews 4:16)

Prayer

'Father,

There are some of us who feel you have not been answering some of our prayers. We understand that it may be unidentified or unconfessed sin which is hindering the operation of your Spirit in our lives.

It may be:
– our critical spirits,
– unforgiveness,
– indiscipline,
– idolatry,
– broken promises,
– disobedience,
– unbelief,
– lack of submission, or other things.

Show us where the blockages lie, so that we might be free and be able to hear you clearly once more and willingly, spontaneously, respond to your every desire for us.

In Jesus name, Amen.'

Endnotes

1. Evelyn Christenson, *What Happens When Women Pray.* Wheaton, Illinois: Victor Books, 1975, 23–25.
2. Dick Eastman, *No Easy Road.* Grand Rapids, Michigan: Baker Book House, 1971, 33.
3. R. Earl Allen, 'Quotable', *Ministries Today*, July/August 1997, 16.
4. Jim Graham, *Prayer.* London, Scripture Union, 1985, 23.
5. Breige McKenna, *Miracles Do Happen.* London: Pan Books, 1987, 22–23.
6. Charles Mahaney, 'Why Don't I Pray More?' *Pastoral Renewal*, April, 1986, 145–147.
7. Evelyn Christenson, *What Happens When Woman Pray.* Wheaton, Illinois: Victor Books, 1975, 55–56.

Chapter 7

Unanswered Prayer

(Psalm 94:9)

'Most Americans say prayers every day, even though no one knows why only some are answered.' [1]

One of the most exciting stories in the whole Bible is found in 1 Kings 18. The prophet Elijah was on top on Mount Carmel. Before him on the altar lay two bulls ready for sacrifice. All morning the 450 priests of Baal had chanted, danced and begged their god to let fire fall from heaven and thus prove that he was greater than Jehovah. The heavens were singularly unimpressed. Nothing had happened.

When Elijah stepped forward he requested that the whole altar and the wood around be soaked with water, not once but three times. When everything was drenched he stepped forward and called out to God to answer his prayer by fire. Immediately the fire of the Lord fell and burned up the sacrifice, the wood, the stones, the water and even the surrounding soil. Then:

> 'When all the people saw this they fell prostrate and cried, "The Lord, he is God! The Lord, he is God!"'

(1 Kings 18:39)

How exciting it is to find God dramatically answering prayer instantly. It's just as exciting when something like that happens today.

A Muslim convert to Christianity received a phone call as

he worked in his government office, advising him that fire had broken out near his home which looked as if it would soon be destroyed. He rushed home and had time only to remove a few of his possessions.

Then, unable to do anything else he stood outside his soon to be burned home, and while his Muslim neighbours who had been so hostile towards him watched, he raised his hands and his voice toward heaven and called out in a loud voice asking God to save his home. No sooner had he concluded, **'In Jesus name, Amen!'**, than the thunder clapped and rain poured down from heaven extinguishing the flames.[2]

His erstwhile persecutors were certainly impressed by his seemingly new relationship with the Almighty.

And we would be too. How marvellous it is when God dramatically, supernaturally, instantly answers prayer.

On the other hand, I received news recently regarding another Muslim convert. He had been caught by his neighbours who demanded he forsake his new found Christian faith. He refused. So they commenced to torture him by cutting off his fingers. Still he would not deny his new faith so they cut off his hands and tied him to a tree and left him overnight. When they returned the next morning he was dead. By the time the press arrived to report the story, the corpse had been hung from a tree and reporters were told that this person was so ashamed that he had left the Muslim faith that he had committed suicide by hanging himself!

What happened here?

Did this man or some of his new friends not pray?

If they did, did God turn a deaf ear and choose not to act?

Doesn't the Bible say, *'Call to me and I will answer you and show you great and mighty things which you do not know'* (Jeremiah 33:3)?

Didn't Jesus say, *'Whatever things you ask when you pray, believe that you receive them and you will have them'* (Mark 11:24)?

Didn't Jesus further say, *'If two or three of you agree on earth concerning anything that they ask it will be done for them by my Father in heaven'* (Matthew 18:19)?

Didn't the apostle John record Jesus as saying, *'The Father will give you anything you ask in my name'* (John 16:23)?

Because there are so many seemingly broad, sweeping, almost unlimited precious promises studded throughout the Scriptures can I not as some suggest simply 'name it and claim it'?

If this is so why is it that we also read, see, hear and experience ourselves, with a degree of frustrating frequency that God does **not** seem to answer prayer?

Mind you, in this regard we're in excellent company.

One of the finest men, the noblest of gentleman who ever walked the earth, was a fellow by the name of Job. He was a totally deserving, God-fearing man. And yet he went from prosperity to poverty, from riches to rags, from health to disease.

The greatest king Israel ever had was David. In the book of Acts we read that, *'David was a man after God's own heart'* (Acts 13:22). But when his baby was dying David lay on the ground and prayed and prayed and begged God for the boy's life. But God let the boy die.[3]

In the New Testament there was Paul, the church's greatest all-time missionary. His ministry was full of words, works and wonders (2 Corinthians 12:12). If anyone had a good connection with God it was Paul. He did amazing things. Yet when he asked God for a favour to release him from a troubling affliction, nothing happened. Obviously God considered in Paul's case that it was better he remained weakened and dependent rather than independent; that it was better that he remain humbled than healed.[4]

For that matter, in any gathering of believers there are so many who have prayed to find a job, but still have found none. Prayer unanswered?

There are so many parents who have prayed for their children who won't listen and who insist on treading wayward, dangerous paths through life. Prayer unanswered?

There are so many students who have asked God to help them with exams and yet they have tasted failure. Prayer unanswered?

There are so many people who have seen their loved ones struggle with disease and begged God for their lives but they have died. Prayer unanswered?

Some have seen loved ones killed in accidents after they have asked for God's protection. Prayer unanswered?

There are so many singles who have begged God for a spouse and yet in spite of the finest quality of their lives nothing has happened. Prayer unanswered?

There are so many children who have prayed for parents and yet the violence and abuse have continued. Prayer unanswered?

And there are others, who for years have prayed for spouses and other close relatives to come into the Kingdom of God and they are still outside. Prayer unanswered?

– How do we respond to this situation?
– Do we try to deny it?
– Do we try to ignore it?
– Do we try to bail God out?

Often times in the stunning silence of disappointment ceaseless questions reverberate around the empty chamber of our tired minds. 'Why? What have I done? How else could I have prayed? Why this? Is there no answer?'

Only very gradually do we start to appreciate that God is not a celestial banker on which we can cash in our promissory notes.[5] He is not a cosmic bellboy or super servant running to do our bidding. He is not an extraterrestrial vending machine in which we put in a coin and out pops a refreshing sparkling answer. How do we cope with this?

So the questions are put:

> *'Why, O Lord, do you stand far off?*
> *Why do you hide yourself in times of trouble?'*
>
> (Psalm 10:1)

> *'Why do you hold back your right hand?*
> *. . . Why don't you destroy my enemies?'*
>
> (Psalm 74:11)

> *'Does he who implanted the ear not hear?'* (Psalm 94:9)

Reasons

In my own grappling with this age-old mystery I have come across in excess of twenty reasons it may seem that God is not responding to our prayer. Let's touch on six of the commonest.

1. Sin

The commonest cause for seeming unanswered prayer is sin somewhere on the scene.

When Israel's army commander-in-chief, Joshua, was pleading with God for a military victory after the crushing defeat at Ai, it was denied him (Joshua 7).

In the toughest way God had to teach his people that more than anything else they had to be obedient to him, otherwise they would end up as little more than a nameless band of ill-disciplined, plundering marauders. Sin was in their midst and it had to be rooted out and dealt with. And until that happened they could expect continued disaster.[6]

Similarly, when King David begged with God to save his son, God seemed not to answer. David had sinned. He then tried to use prayer as a crutch to evade the consequences of his own sin. God would have none of it (2 Samuel 12:16–22).

Later he could say:

> *'If I had cherished sin in my heart,*
> *the Lord would not have listened.'* (Psalm 66:18)

Isaiah put it thus:

> *'Your sin has separated you from God ... so that he will not*
> *hear you.'* (Isaiah 59:1–2)

Sin separates and silences God. It's the first thing we always have to examine on our check list if prayer is seemingly unanswered.

2. Selfishness

A more subtle yet equally common cause for unanswered prayer is selfishness.

It is true that:

> '*My God will supply all your needs.*'   (Philippians 4:19)

But a wants/wish list is not a needs list. James wrote:

> '*When you ask you do not receive because you ask with wrong motives that you may spend what you get on your pleasures.*'
> (James 4:3)

Simply evoking the name of Jesus in a prayer does not automatically oblige God to answer. The question is, what are our motives behind the prayer?

We may ask God to help us get rich, so that we can help the poor. But our real motive may be we simply like money, so that we can buy a luxury car or a second home.

We may ask God for good weather and say that we are praying thus to help farmers and their crops. But our real motive may be that we only want to enjoy a good holiday.

We might pray asking God to bring judgment on sin because we know that God hates sin. But our personal motive is to get at some sinners who are hassling us.[7]

We might pray for a Prime Minister or a President, because the Bible commands us to pray for those in authority over us (1 Timothy 2:1–2). But our real motive may be that we pray for them because they are members of our political party and we want to see them whip the opposition.

When we are younger we pray for members of the opposite sex that they might be saved because we know that God wants all people everywhere to be saved (2 Peter 3:9). However our real motive may be self-centred because we want to marry that person.

We certainly have a tendency to try to avoid any form of suffering even though Paul encouraged otherwise.

> '*We are to rejoice in our sufferings because we know that suffering produces perseverance; perseverance produces character; and character hope. And hope does not disappoint us, because love is poured out into our hearts by the Holy Spirit, whom he has given us.*'
> (Romans 5:3–5)

But when was the last time we welcomed and rejoiced at the onset of suffering? See how subtle our motives are. If our motives are self-centred, then probably are prayers may seem to go unanswered.

3. Stinginess

A third reason for seemingly unanswered prayer and one which is so common is our own stinginess. The Bible says:

> *'If a man shuts his ears to the cry of the poor, he too will cry out and not be answered.'*   (Proverbs 21:13)

Many Christians love to quote Philippians where it says:

> *'My God will meet all your needs according to his glorious riches in Christ Jesus.'*   (Philippians 4:19)

But that promise is placed within the context of generosity toward others. We cannot expect God to be meeting our needs unless we are generous toward the needs of others. The Bible is quite clear on this principle.

George Mueller was a man whom God used mightily through prayer. It was so, in part, because whatever Mueller was receiving, he was constantly passing on to others. The Bible is quite clear on this principle:

> *'Give, and it will be given to you ... for with the measure you use, it will be measured to you.'*   (Luke 6:38)

> *'We receive from him anything we ask.'*   (1 John 3:22)

What a marvellous statement! But again that statement is in the context of generously giving to the needs of others. If God knows we are not going to be generous toward others, not only will he not be giving to us, but he may not even be answering us. He gives in proportion to the degree to which he can trust us to pass it on. And the same may be true of the degree to which he is prepared to answer our prayers.

Last century for 60 years George Mueller housed and fed up to 2000 orphans at a time. There were never any appeals.

There were no collections. Yet he prayed in millions and millions of pounds. How could God answer such prayers?

We get a clue to the heart of this man through his death. When he died there was just enough left in his accounts to pay for his funeral and no more. In other words, God could trust this man. None of the monies which God gave through him ever stuck to his fingers. The next time we pray for God to be meeting our financial needs consider what is our record in the books of heaven regarding giving to God's Kingdom.

4. Relationships

A fourth very common reason for seemingly unanswered prayer is found in the area of relationships, especially within marriage. If any husband or wife has a relationship with each other which is anything less than the best which God desires, then prayer is affected. God will not be hearing and answering so clearly if that relationship is impaired. The Bible says quiet clearly to husbands that they are to be,

> '...considerate toward their wives and treat them with respect as heirs of the gracious gift of life, so that nothing will hinder your prayers.'　　　　　(1 Peter 3:7)

Husbands may be active in Christian work and admired within the church. Wives may be devoted to the church and faithful in attendance and have a very good reputation. But if we are out of sorts with each other so that our marriage is less than God desires, then deadness and powerlessness in prayer will result. Husbands and wives need to bring the whole of their married life before God and allow him to sort things out.

5. Timing

A fifth reason for seemingly unanswered prayer is that of timing. The writer of Hebrews said:

> 'Do not throw away your confidence; it will be richly rewarded. You need to persevere so that when you have done the will of God, you will receive what he has promised.'
> 　　　　　(Hebrews 10:35–36)

To which James adds:

> *'Consider it pure joy, my brothers, whenever you face trials of*
> *many kinds because you know that the testing of your faith*
> *develops perseverance. Perseverance must finish its work so*
> *that you may be mature and complete not lacking anything.'*
>
> (James 1:2–4)

God is interested in bringing us to maturity and that process can seldom be accelerated.

When the promise of a child was given to Abram and Sarai (Genesis 15), it was many decades before that promise was fulfilled. The timing delay was to stress and highlight the fact that the birth of the boy Isaac was no natural event. It was supernatural as a special gift from God.[8]

When the sisters appealed to Jesus because his friend Lazarus was dying, Jesus deliberately delayed. Lazarus died. Was he being callous and uncaring? No. The event was such that it wasn't to be just a healing of Lazarus from sickness but that Lazarus would be called forth from death after he had been dead for days. The delayed timing was meant to demonstrate that Jesus had power not only over sickness but over death itself (John 11).

Before my wife and I came to Melbourne, she had a growth on her thumb. That growth was cut out by surgeons. It was medicated by physicians. It was frozen by refrigeration experts. It was herbalised by herbal specialists. It was even de-demonised by specialists in deliverance ministry. But nothing permanently removed that growth. Then one day after 10 years as we were struggling to discern whether or not God was calling us from our ministry overseas to come to Melbourne, something happened.

In a moment of jest when my wife asked me what would it take to convince me that God was in this call I said, 'If God would remove that growth from your thumb I would believe.' She departed on a train journey to another country to take our children back to school. Six days later when she returned, she reminded me of my jest. I asked to see the thumb. She showed it to me and I claimed that she was showing me the wrong thumb. She showed me the other thumb. We ran out of other thumbs.

She later told me that when I spoke those words, as she left me, immediately that growth started to slough off her thumb and was replaced by beautiful, new, baby-like skin. For 10 years God had kept that growth there for a special occasion to speak loudly to me.

Wait for the timing of God.

But the sixth reason for seemingly unanswered prayer is the commonest and most difficult to understand.

6. Simply the Best

One of the most comforting verses in the Bible says:

> *We know that in all things God works for the good of those who love him, who have been called according to his purpose.'*
> (Romans 8:28).

To which Paul later adds:

> *God is working in us both to will and to do his good pleasure.'*
> (Philippians 2:13)

In other words God is always looking out for what is in our own long-term best interest.

Some years ago American pop singer Tina Turner had a great hit. In Australia it was even adopted as a national theme song for rugby league football. The title of her song was 'Simply the Best'. That's the way it is with God. We ask for something yet he chooses not to grant it because he wants to give us something else which is 'simply the best'.

When Peter, James and John were on the Mount of Transfiguration it is recorded how they suddenly saw Moses and Elijah appearing with Jesus (Matthew 17:1–13). They figured this was the best and immediately wanted to erect a shelter to stay right there. But Jesus didn't agree because there was something even better than this. He descended down onto the plain and went to his crucifixion, resurrection and ascension. Certainly for us, not for him, this was something much better.

During the 1980s when the need was first realised for our Church to relocate, we searched everywhere for land. We turned up at a public auction of a large block of land. On that day we bid two and a quarter million dollars even though we didn't have a cent in the bank. We were beaten by another party. We were depressed. We were discouraged. We were confused. It took us about another five years to work through the difficulties existent in our church at that time and then God led us to where we are now, undoubtedly a site without parallel. But we could not know that at the time.

Again when I was being called back from work overseas to my current position in Melbourne, for months and months I struggled with leaving that former work. I figured that God was throwing me out onto the scrap heap, that I was the most useless sinner that there ever was. Why else would he order me back to Australia? What I couldn't understand at the time was that one of the reasons that it was better for me to leave that work was so that it could explode into growth many hundreds of times greater than may have been possible had I remained there. And of course, he wanted me to be a part of something new in Australia as well.

What if God had answered my prayers in my younger days that I become a lion tamer? By this time I could have ended up as chunks of meat inside a can of pet food.

What if God had answered my prayer to become a driver of a steam train? I would have been redundant by now.

What if God had answered my prayer that I would become a soldier? I could have been dead and rotting in the fields of some war zone.

God often denies our prayer so that he can give us a better answer even though it may take many years for us to understand that.

Our problem is that we are down in the midst of circumstances and cannot lift our vision too high.

In 1994 during the fiftieth anniversary of the landing of allied troops on the shores of France, in the Second World War, two interviews were recorded. One was of a former soldier who was fighting at ground level. He said, 'I was convinced that there was no way that we could possibly win the battle.' The second interview was with a pilot who had been high overhead. He said, 'From my perspective I was convinced that there was no way that we could possibly lose the battle.'

Similarly, God always has a better vantage point than we do.

> *'As the heavens are higher than the earth,*
> *so are my ways higher than your ways*
> *and my thoughts higher than your thoughts.'*

(Isaiah 55:9)

The ultimate issue at stake is not whether we get what we want when we want it but whether or not we will continue to trust in God and to believe that he is good and kind and generous and continues to want to give us the best. Faith is not so much summed up in the answers God gives. It is in our response to him when he seems not to give answers.

When he chooses to remain silent, faith rests content.

If he seems to choose to say 'No', we need to remain grateful that he cares enough to give us such a tough answer. In our infantile attitudes we need to remember that often we are too immature to read the road signs of life and too small to see what lies ahead.[9]

The book of Revelation records the response of a people who entered into adversity. It says that they cursed God (Revelation 1:22).

On the other hand in the Old Testament there is recorded the story of Job. When God permitted Job to suffer so terribly Jobs response was:

> *'Naked I came from my mother's womb,*
> *and naked I will depart.*
> *The Lord gave and the Lord has taken away;*
> *may the name of the Lord be praised.'* (Job 1:21)

And then it goes on to say:

> *'...Job did not sin by charging God with wrong doing.'*

(Job 1:22)

What is the choice of our response to seemingly un-answered prayer?

Such is a God-given opportunity to grow in faith. Stumbling blocks of doubt become stepping stones to great faith and intimacy with God.

The Psalmist asked the questions:

> *'Will the Lord reject forever?*
> *Will he never show his favour again?*
> *Has his unfailing love vanished forever?*
> *Has his promise failed for all time?*
> *Has God forgotten to be merciful?*
> *Has his anger withheld compassion?** (Psalm 77:7–9)

Then gives an answer:

> *'I will remember the deeds of the Lord:*
> *Yes, I will remember your miracles of long ago.'*
> (Psalm 77:11)

> *'... as for me, I will always have hope;*
> *I will praise you more and more.'* (Psalm 71:14)

Endnotes

1. Kenneth L. Woodward, 'Is God Listening', *Newsweek*, April 1, 1997, 81.
2. Leith Anderson, *When God Says No*. Minneapolis, Minnesota: Bethany House Publishers, 1996, 9.
3. Leith Anderson, *When God Says No*. Minneapolis, Minnesota: Bethany House Publishers, 1996, 9.
4. *Ibid.*, 16.
5. *Ibid.*, 134.
6. Helen Grace Lescheid, 'Ten Questions to Ask When Your Prayers are Unanswered', *Discipleship Journal*, Issue sixty-eight, 1992, 49.
7. R.E.O. White, 'When God Says "No"', *Australian Baptist*, May 25, 1988, 6.
8. Anderson, *When God Says No*. 144.
9. Wilkinson, 'Unanswered Prayer – A Trial of Faith', *New Life*, March 11, 1993.
10. Anderson, *When God Says No*. 99.

Chapter 8

Warfare

(Ephesians 6:10–20)

On the 23rd of January, 1997 a fax arrived in my office. It had come in overnight from an international missions head-quarters office in London. They had received news of one of their medical missionaries who was giving a deputation talk in Michigan, in the United States. This missionary worked in Africa.

At the meeting in the church he was telling people how he travelled every two weeks by bicycle through the jungle to a nearby city for supplies. This required him to camp out overnight halfway. On one of those trips he saw two men fighting in the city where he bought his medicine. One was seriously injured, so he treated him and witnessed to him about Jesus Christ. He then returned home without incident. He continues the story as follows:

> 'Upon arriving in the city several weeks later, I was approached by the man I had treated earlier. He told me that he had known that I was carrying money and medicine. He said, "Some friends and I followed you into the jungle knowing you would camp overnight. We waited for you to go to sleep and planned to kill you and take your money and drugs. Just as we were about to go into your camp site, we saw that you were surrounded by twenty-six armed guards."

I laughed at this and said I was certainly alone out in the jungle camp site. But the young man pressed the point, "No sir, I was not the only one to see the guards. My friends also saw them and we all counted them. There were twenty-six. It was because of those twenty-six guards that we were afraid and left you alone." '

At this point in the church presentation in Michigan a man jumped up and interrupted the missionary and asked, 'Can you tell me the exact date when this happened?' The missionary thought for a while and recalled the date. Then the man in the congregation told his side of the story.

'On that night in Africa it was morning here. I was preparing to play golf. As I put my bags in the car, I felt the Lord leading me to pray for you. In fact, the urging was so strong that I called the men of this church together to pray for you. Will all of those men who met with me that day, please stand?'

The men who had met that day to pray together stood. There were twenty-six of them.

The apostle Paul said:

'Our struggle is not against flesh and blood, but against the rulers, against the authorities, against the powers of this dark world and against the spiritual forces of evil in the heavenly realms.'   (Ephesians 6:12)

Because of this he went on to say:

'Pray in the Spirit on all occasions with all kinds of prayers and requests. With this in mind, be alert and always keep on praying for all the saints. Pray also for me.'
(Ephesians 6:18)

Around the world believers are starting to take seriously Paul's invitation to enter spiritual warfare through prayer.

An underground chamber dubbed 'the war room' is being built in the foothills of the Rocky Mountains, near Colorado Springs (USA). The war room is modelled on military command centres and is to be officially known as the World Prayer Centre. It will soon be the home of a special group dedicated to praying about the various world crises that confront us all. 'This is not a come-and-have-fun-prayer room,' says Ted Haggard, pastor of the New Life Church in Colorado Springs and the driving force behind the $7 million centre. This will be a strategic nerve centre for global, evangelistic prayer.[1]

The people of the world who live in the toughest spiritual bondage are across northern Africa, the Middle East and Asia. This is the heartland of the strongest non-Christian religions of Hinduism, Buddhism, Islam and others. 95% of the least evangelised people in the world live in these countries.

But in 1992 a call went out for a million prayer warriors (intercessors) to focus on this part of the globe (known as the 10/40 Window). 20 million intercessors responded from 105 countries. By October 1995, the number of people praying had risen to 36.7 million. A spiritual battle has been engaged using the weapon of prayer to liberate spiritual captives.

The result?

In some African nations, the church is growing at twice the rate of local population gains. In China, it is suggested Christians may now number 100 million, a quarter of whom have come to faith only in the last four years. Because too many Communists were becoming Christians, the Communist Party circularised its members reminding them they are supposed to be atheists.

In one radically resistant country when a sole believer of a village died, he was buried in a cemetery outside the village. His neighbours later saw a stranger leave the cemetery, walk into the village and look into many of the houses. That same day the village was also visited by some Christians who showed the *Jesus* film. As the villagers saw Jesus on the screen they exclaimed, 'That's the man we saw going from house to house.' They all came to believe in him. In that same country, 15,000 new believers are being baptised each day.[2]

Raju is a new Christian who has personally experienced the miraculous physical healing of a tumour. As he passed

through a village in Rajastan in North West India, he heard
that a local politician, who was a fanatical Hindu, had just
died. Raju offered to pray for the dead man, but the dead
man's relatives urged him to go away. Ignoring them, Raju
pushed through the crowd, placed his hands on the dead
man's body and unsheathed his weapon of prayer against the
most powerful enemy – death. As he prayed, the dead man's
hands started to move. People were frightened. But Raju
instructed everyone to declare that 'Jesus is Lord' while he
battled on in prayer.

As everyone confessed Jesus as Saviour, the dead man
returned to life. Consequently all the politician's family
decided to become Christians.

But others reported the matter to the police as a breach of
the anti-conversion law. When the police arrived to make
arrests, they were asked to wait because the prayer meeting
was still in progress. That same day 350 previously orthodox
Hindus were baptised, all because a believer prayed and death
was defeated.[3]

As believers through prayer engage in battle, God works.

Clearly, if God is going to do something in any nation and
we are to be useful to him, then we have to tap in to the
greatest resource in our spiritual armoury, the launching
weapon of prayer.

To pray is not the only thing we can do, but it is probably
the greatest thing. Someone has said, 'The devil trembles
when he sees God's weakest child upon his knees.'

1. Why Pray?

We pray because Jesus has commanded it.

(a) A command

Jesus said:

> *'Ask . . . seek . . . knock.'*   (Matthew 7:7–8)

If the kingdom of darkness is prevailing, it is because few
are withstanding it in the name of Jesus.

Someone has said:

> 'God's is the power.
> Ours is the prayer.
> Without him we cannot.
> Without us he will not.'

Prayer is a means of power by which the church is meant to do its work. God has appointed us to a sacred partnership for the purpose of advancing his kingdom. In part, we have been created to pray.

The apostle Peter said believers are a *'holy and royal priesthood'* (1 Peter2:9). Part of the privilege of being priests is that we will be interceding for others in their situation.

Secondly, we pray because compassion compels it.

(b) Compassion

When Paul Yonggi Cho was asked why so many of his people went to Prayer Mountain to fast and pray when they could have been spending their time doing other things, he said:

> 'If you, or members of your family were dying of cancer and you knew there was a cure, wouldn't you do whatever was necessary to produce healing? Many people are suffering from both physical and spiritual cancer. Material prosperity does not bring happiness and fulfilment. We have discovered that people's needs are met when we are totally dedicated to prayer and fasting.' [4]

When Jesus looked out on to the vast harvest fields of humanity, *'He had compassion on them...'* (Matthew 9:36).

With that in mind, he commanded his disciples to pray.

As people commit themselves to pray, things begin to happen.

From the pages of the Bible we learn how God unleashes his angels to rush to the assistance of his people when they pray (2 Kings 6:15–17; Daniel 10:13; Hebrews 1:14). We also see how Satan's hold is broken, his hindrances are overcome and his work is destroyed.

Christ enforces Calvary's victory through the prayers of his church. If either through obedience or compassion we ought to pray and we don't, then why don't we?

2. Why Don't We Pray?

There are at least four reasons. The first is:

(a) Lack of Understanding

Some may say, 'It's because we haven't understood. We haven't had enough teaching.'

Many of us don't understand electricity, but we flick a switch to warm ourselves, to give us light, to watch television or to cook our food. Most of us don't understand the principles of an internal combustion engine, yet we turn the key and drive our cars. We enjoy these things. We don't have to understand everything about God to talk to or listen to him.

Prayer is to the soul what breathing is to the body. It is done whether we understand it or not.

A second reason for not praying may be discouragement.

(b) Discouragement

Some may say, 'Well, I used to pray and I didn't see much happening so I gave up. I guess I got discouraged.'

That's a common experience. But the Bible commands us that we are to go on and persevere in prayer.

A third reason for prayerlessness, may be lack of compassion.

(c) Lack of Compassion

God is *'not wanting anyone to perish, but everyone to come to repentance'* (2 Peter 3:9). Maybe some of us have what could be called the 'Jonah syndrome'.

In the book of Jonah there is the story of God wanting the great ancient city of Nineveh to cease its wickedness and to return to him. He commissioned his prophet Jonah to go to warn and to preach to them.

> *'But Jonah ran away from the Lord and headed for Tarshish.*
> *He went down to Joppa where he found a ship bound for that*
> *port. After paying the fare, he went aboard and sailed to*
> *Tarshish to flee from the Lord.'*   (Jonah 3:3)

In other words Jonah did not want to go to Nineveh. He did not want those people to be saved from God's wrath.

When Jonah finally obeyed, the people of the city heard him. They turned back to God. Then God *'had compassion and did not bring upon them the destruction he had threatened'* (Jonah 3:10). But, *'...Jonah was greatly displeased and became angry'* (Jonah 4:1). How many of us are like Jonah and almost wish that God would wipe out people because to us they seem unredeemable. We lack compassion.

A fourth reason for not praying could be laziness or busyness.

(d) Laziness or Busyness

Elsewhere I have mentioned the testimonies of George Mahaney and David Watson who respectively through laziness and busyness lacked the motivation to do what God requires of us. If we are to achieve power in prayer, then discipline will be essential. If we make an appointment with God, then we must turn up for that appointment.

Prayer is not a matter of time so much as priority. We always have time for what is important to us. And if we say we are too busy to spend quality time with God in prayer, then we are busier than God means us to be. Prayer is a calling of God upon us all and not just an option for the zealous few.

If this is so, what are we to do?

3. What To Do?

Firstly, we should ask for a desire to pray.

(a) Ask for Desire

If we are spiritually listless and rarely hunger for time with God, if we are low on patience and compassion to where prayer, such as it may be, has become a duty rather than a joy; if our worship lacks spontaneity and our participation in the life of the church has become half-hearted, then we need to ask God to rekindle a desire for himself within us.

We are encouraged to press on, to know the Lord (Hosea 6:3).

Paul says:

> *'I consider everything a loss compared to the surpassing greatness of knowing Christ Jesus my Lord ... I want to know Christ and the power of his resurrection.'*
>
> (Philippians 3:8, 10)

What is our deepest desire? If it is not to know God, to experience the reality of his presence, to commune with him, to prevail with him – then we need to ask God to rekindle that desire within us. As he grants that, then we learn to pray by praying.

The more we pray, the more we will want to pray and the easier it will become to hear and to know the voice of the Lord.

The next thing we need to do is to persevere.

(b) Persevere

As we start, remember we are not to grow weary. It may take years for the full answers to come. But,

> *'Let us not become weary in doing good, for at the proper time we will reap a harvest if we do not give up.'* (Galatians 6:9)

To pray is a good thing. As we commence to move in this area we need some guidelines to help us along the way.

4. Guidelines

Guideline number one is to remember the battle.

(a) Remember the Battle

We need to remember always that we are in a battle.

> *'For though we live in the world, we do not wage war as the world does. The weapons we fight with are not the weapons of the world. On the contrary they have divine power to demolish strongholds.'*
> (2 Corinthians 10:3–4)

Prayer is one of those vehicles to launch the weapons. Secondly we are to take our authority.

(b) Take Authority

Jesus said:

> *'I have given you authority.'*
> (Luke 10:19)

Elsewhere he said to Peter:

> *'I give you the keys of the kingdom.'* (Matthew 16:19)

Later he extended that authority to other believers saying that whatever we bind on earth will be bound in heaven and whatever we loose on earth will be loosed in heaven. Whenever two or three come together in his name, he is with them (Matthew 18:18–20).

As we harmonise on anything that we ask, he will do it.

The staggering thing is that we seem to be given responsibility for what happens in the heavenlies. If only we can grasp that!

Often we think we are waiting for God to act. But many times the reverse may be the truth. He may be waiting for us to act.

Thirdly, we need to identify the strongman.

(c) Identify the Strongman

Referring to driving out demons by the Spirit of God, Jesus uses the analogy of entering a strongman's house. But before anything is achieved he notes, that one first needs to tie up the strongman (Matthew 12:28–29).

Paul said:

> *'I do not run like a man running aimlessly, I do not fight like a man beating the air.'* (1 Corinthians 9:26)

We are not to waste time in generalities. We need to wait on God to understand the specifics of the nature of the real opposition.

In Argentina, evangelist Omar Cabrera waits on God through prayer and fasting to understand the nature of the spiritual authorities over a city, before he goes in to preach. He says that unless we do this it is like putting on a great banquet outside the walls of a goal and inviting the prisoners within to participate.

Anyone who has been near Argentinian prisons knows that often the prisoners try to hang out through the windows. They wave to passers by. They call out and whistle. But they cannot escape.

Cabrera says that the Gospel is like a banquet. For prisoners to be free to participate, the walls have to come down. When he prays and fasts along with others, and understands the nature of the 'strongman' by the authority which he has in Jesus, those walls are cast down. Then as he preaches, people 'drop' into the kingdom like ripe fruit falling from a tree.

Fourthly, we need to pray God's will.

(d) Pray God's Will

Before we pray concerning our desires, we must understand what God's desires are and let them shape our own. If we do not do this, when we pray we only reinforce our own self-centredness.

> *'This is the assurance we have in approaching God that if we ask anything according to his will he hears us.'*
>
> (John 5:14–15)

What are some of the things that we could pray which we know are: 'according to his will?'

We can pray for:
- The building up of his church
- Growth, blessing, unity, vision
- Giving, tithing
- Increased prayer power
- Revival, labourers in God's harvest

- The harvest itself
- Salvation of people
- The blessing of God on the nation
- Home and family, government, leadership
- The restraint of Satan.

These are all areas which are directly in line with God's will as revealed to us in the Bible.

Fifthly, we must remember to persevere.

(e) Persevere

Jesus told a story about the person who was desperate to borrow three loaves of bread during the night, and he summed it up by comparing that man's persistence and our attitude as we come in prayer to God (Luke 11:5–13).

Jesus went on to say:

> *'So I say to you: ask and it will be given to you; seek and you will find; knock and the door will be opened unto you.'*
>
> (Luke 11:9)

Do not give up! Do not give in! Continue the offensive until victory is won.

God once said to Joshua, *'Hold out toward Ai the javelin that is in your hand'* (Joshua 8:18) so, *'... Joshua did not draw back the hand that held out his javelin until he had destroyed all who lived in Ai'* (Joshua 8:26).

The javelin did nothing militarily. But in the spiritual realm Joshua was laying hold of God's promise to give them that city, claiming it, persevering, until it was fulfilled.

(f) Pray in the Spirit

Finally, within the context of spiritual warfare Paul says in Ephesians, *'Pray in the Spirit on all occasions'* (Ephesians 6:18). Why?

Often we don't know how to pray. Our minds don't give us the insight that we need. But,

> *'The Spirit helps us in our weakness. We do not know what we ought to pray for, but the Spirit himself intercedes for us*

*with groans that words cannot express . . . the Spirit intercedes
for the saints in accordance with God's will.'*

(Romans 8:26–27)

In other words, he knows the will of God for every person
in every situation. When we pray 'in the Spirit', we will
therefore surely invade the impossible and penetrate the
impenetrable with Holy Spirit energy. If God has gifted us
with a special prayer language, then we ought to use it. We
need to allow the Holy Spirit to use us in prevailing prayer.

Knowing about prayer will never take the place of prayer
itself. If we fail to pray, we are telling God that what he has
begun in the Spirit we can finish in the flesh. If we fail to
pray, then in practice we are atheists. We need to talk less
and do more regarding the matter of prayer.

John Wesley of England used to say,

> 'God is limited by only two things: unbelief and lack of
> prayer.'

In 1905 John Hyde believed that God was laying it upon
his heart to pray one person into the kingdom of God each
day throughout that year. The next year, after he had
confessed the smallness of his faith and his petitions, he
was led to pray for two people a day. Before the end of that
year, just over eight hundred people had joined the church.
During the last year of his life, his faith and persistence was
still being honoured as he prayed for four people a day to
come into the kingdom of God.[5]

> *'The prayer of a righteous man is powerful and effective.'*
>
> (James 5:16)

If we want to be strong in battle and want to see God do
great things in his church and the nation, then we need to
ask, are we ready to take on the responsibility of the extraordinary prayer which is required of us all?

If that is so, then we won't avoid taking on an extra
guideline of prayer linked with **fasting**.

Endnotes

1. C. Peter Wagner, 'Message from the President', *AD2000 United Prayer Track Brochure*, n.d.
2. Praying Through the Window 111, *The Unreached Peoples*, The Christian Information Network, Colorado Springs, USA.
3. *Dawn Friday* – fax, 97/20, via e-mail.
4. Paul Y. Cho, *Prayer: Key to Revival*. Herts, England: Word Publishing, 1985, 14.
5. 'Great Men of Prayer', *Restore*, April 1993, 13.

Chapter 9

Tough Stuff – Fasting[1]
(Matthew 6:16–18)

In a south Asian city when a missionary saw a cow about to be slaughtered in front of a mosque, he stopped his car, took a few pictures, then drove home. But that night the Holy Spirit began to challenge him to be less of a tourist and more a missionary. He was directed to commence praying and fasting, to return to the scene of the sacrifice and to be a witness to the greater sacrifice of Jesus.

In the steaming pre-monsoon heat of the next day, he set off with his shoulder bag full of tracts and gospels to the same place in the bazaar, where he had taken pictures the preceding day near the mosque. Having sold and distributed much, as he returned home he felt well satisfied that he had done 'his duty'.

But again the Holy Spirit impressed upon him that night to continue praying and fasting and to return to repeat the process in the same place the next day. Night after night as the missionary continued to pray and fast, the Holy Spirit repeated his instruction.

It didn't take long for local opposition to realise what was happening. A somewhat angry group formed and waited for him in the bazaar and threatened to take his life. He was dragged through the market place, doused in dye, kicked and pushed into a dirty ditch and stoned. Twice a fanatic tried to kill him with a dagger, but was restrained by his own people.

Finally, two well trained trouble-makers were appointed to stop his witnessing. They warned him that if he returned to the bazaar, he would not leave there alive.

On the fortieth day of this supernaturally sustained period of prayer and fasting, directed by what the Spirit was saying, he bade farewell to his wife realising he might never see her again. No sooner had he arrived in the bazaar than the trouble-makers showed up. They tore his gospels and tracts to pieces and began to stir up the growing crowd which quickly gathered to watch the spectacle. Soon there were calls to kill him.

Then just as men moved in to grab him, two unusually tall strangers appeared. Spearing a path through the crowd which was now calling for the missionary's blood, in one swift move they grabbed him, removed him from the crush of people and took him down a lane at the end of which was a waiting cycle rickshaw.

Amazingly, no one followed them.

Placing the missionary in the rickshaw, the unusual stranger said to him 'It is enough for now. Don't come back.'

God's messengers had saved his servant. That night the Lord spoke to him once more saying, 'Now you know how much I love and care for Muslims. It is not my will that any of them should perish without hearing the message of salvation.'

With no other resources other than the practice of sustained prayer and fasting, that missionary went on to be God's instrument to build what became one of the largest churches in that somewhat hostile environment.

When Christians combine prayer with fasting, powerful spiritual forces seem to be harnessed and then released.

Today however, at least in the western church, fasting is hardly a widespread or spiritual discipline. In fact, there is ample evidence to suggest that the practice of the opposite, overeating, may be more widespread.

While fasting has become a political mechanism in many countries, or even a means of fund-raising for some well-known charities, it is either ignored or mentioned only jokingly in large sections of the church. In others it receives only partial attention in the period prior to Easter. Even though it is acceptable to other religions and sports professionals, in the Christian church it is hardly a widespread practice.

Be that as it may, the Bible still has much to say on the topic of fasting.

By fasting, we mean voluntarily going without food and/or fluids for a period of consecrated prayer.

The Bible is studded with many examples of the practice.

Moses fasted for forty days, twice (Deuteronomy 9:9–18).

Joshua fasted after defeat at Ai (Joshua 7:6).

The entire nation of Israel was called to fast (Judges 20:26 and 1 Samuel 7:6).

From its historical experience, Israel knew that within the context of fasting and prayer, potent victories were won.

King Jehosaphat won a military battle through fasting and prayer without engaging in physical combat (2 Chronicles 20:1–30).

By prayer and fasting Ezra obtained safe passage (Ezra 8:21–23).

Queen Esther was used to transform potential genocide into national salvation, through prayer and fasting (Esther 4:16).

In the Sermon on the Mount Jesus refers to the three interconnected responsibilities of giving, praying and fasting (Matthew 6:1–18).

On each of these Jesus did not say, '**If** you give,' or '**if** you pray,' or '**if** you fast.' He said, '**When** you give ... **when** you pray ... **when** you fast.'

As usual Jesus demonstrated his teaching by his own example. In the gospel of Luke we read that Jesus was *'full of the Holy Spirit'* (Luke 4:1). He then went out into the desert where he prayed and fasted during an encounter with Satan. Afterwards, *'He returned in the power of the Spirit'* (Luke 4:14). He started out 'full' of the Spirit and after praying and fasting, became 'empowered' by the Spirit.

Jesus went on to stress that if we would achieve spiritual breakthroughs we needed both to pray and to fast (Mark 9:29).

Religious leaders of Jesus' time also fasted. So accepted was the practice, that onlookers were surprised when they noticed that on a particular occasion when fasting was expected, Jesus' disciples weren't fasting. Jesus defended them by equating his presence with that of a bridal celebration (Mark 2:18–20). But he also clearly inferred that after his departure his disciples certainly would fast.

The first missionary personnel were identified and commissioned within the context of prayer and fasting (Acts 13:1–3). Leaders were identified and appointed also by prayer and fasting (Acts 14:21–23). Paul was praying and fasting prior to his own commissioning and commencement of ministry (Acts 9:9). Later on, he referred to fasting as a sign of the legitimacy of his missionary ministry (2 Corinthians 6:3–10; 11:23–27).

We can see that throughout the record of biblical history, fasting was a normal practice of God's people. It remained a practice throughout much of the history of the church.

One of the reasons for great revivals in the past was because the people whom God chose both prayed and fasted extensively.

On the Korean scene where the church has grown so remarkably, Pastor Paul Yonggi Cho has said:

'Normally I teach my people to begin to fast for three days. Once they have become accustomed to three-day fasts, they'll be able to fast for seven days; then they will move to ten-day fasts. Some have even gone for forty days...'[2]

So what happens when believers fast?

Firstly, it may be that true fasting is emotionally and spiritually a form of mourning. But this is not to be confused with human sadness. Godly fasting is different.

Jesus said that after his departure his people would fast because as with a bridegroom leaving, there would be sadness

(Matthew 9:15). But that fasting would eventually be replaced by feasting (Revelation 22:17, 20). Fasting which is prompted by the Holy Spirit, helps us to identify with God's grief over the sin and folly of humanity. We are sharing in God's feelings.

Jesus said:

> *'Blessed are they that mourn.'* (Matthew 5:4)

Elsewhere we are promised that there will be, *'beauty for ashes, the oil of joy for mourning, the garment of praise for the Spirit of heaviness'* (Isaiah 61:3).

A couple of years ago as I was praying early one morning, I suddenly realised to what degree my church had been subjected to gossip, ridicule and laughter because we dared to believe that at such a time of national economic depression, God wanted us to do something extraordinary. He wanted us to relocate and quadruple our capacity, which in the end would cost us many millions of dollars. In the midst of such national gloom he was wanting us to plan and prepare for victory and expansion. The problem was, many other Christians when they heard of it, laughed at us.

As I prayed on I started to weep, not so much feeling sorry for myself, but identifying how God feels when any part of his body is so regarded by another. I sensed I was moving into a different realm of the Spirit for the next hour or so. Since those times God has been more than faithful providing for all of our extraordinary needs and continues to trust us to care for more and more of his people.

Secondly, we fast to bring our physical bodies into submission.

Paul said:

> *'I beat my body and make it my slave so that after I have preached to others, I myself will not be disqualified for the prize.'* (1 Corinthians 9:27)

Paul kept his body under subjection. It is said of fire that it is a wonderful servant but a terrible master. The same could be said of our bodies. Each time we fast, we are showing our bodies who is in charge. In effect we are saying, 'Body, stomach, fleshly appetites, you will serve me. I will not be dominated by you.' Paul wrote that:

> *'The sinful nature desires what is contrary to the Spirit, and the Spirit what is contrary to sinful nature. They are in conflict with each other.'*
> (Galatians 5:7)

Intimately connected to our sinful nature is our 'flesh'. It is through our flesh that sin comes enticing us. Fasting deals with two great barriers which are erected by our own carnal natures. These are the self-will of the soul and the insistent self-gratifying appetites of our bodies.

Rightly practised, fasting brings both soul and body into submission to the Holy Spirit. Barriers are broken down, communion is opened up. Fasting does not change God, his purposes, plans or standards. But it does change us.

King David once committed adultery with Bathsheba (2 Samuel 12). As a result of that act a child was conceived and born. But God decreed that the child would die. David commenced and continued to pray and fast. The child died. God did not change, but David certainly did. He came to an attitude of repentance and then God was able to forgive him.

Thirdly, when we fast we ought to expect to be victorious overcomers in the matter upon which our accompanying prayer is focused.

King Jehoshaphat once was faced with a hostile army invading his territory from the east (2 Chronicles 20:1–30). He lacked resources adequate to meet the threat. Therefore,

> *'He proclaimed a fast throughout Judah. He gathered together all the people so that they might ask God's help.'*
> (2 Chronicles 20:3–4)

Jehaziel lead the people in singing and praising God. Israel did not have to engage the enemy in hand to hand contact. The invaders self-destructed. So sweeping and startling was Israel's victory, that no other nation dared to attack them for years to come. Collective fasting was a high priority employed in the spiritual area to gain supremacy in the realm of the physical.

Paul highlights this principle when he says:

> *'The weapons we fight with are not the weapons of the world. On the contrary they have divine power to demolish strong-holds.'* (2 Corinthians 10:4)

His spiritual weapons included united prayer combined with fasting.

When Jesus' disciples asked him why they couldn't be as effective as he was in ministry, he replied that some things are achieved, *'only by prayer and fasting'* (Mark 9:29).

Victory is achieved firstly in the realm of the spiritual and then in the physical.

Fourthly, we fast so that we may be heard in heaven.

When Ezra faced the difficult assignment of leading his people through dangerous territory from their place of exile back to their own land, so that they might know how to proceed and receive God's favour and protection, he proclaimed a fast (Ezra 8:21–23).

The result was that through their long trek through hostile areas, they were neither molested by bandits nor attacked by savage tribes. They suffered no loss of property or persons because they had been heard and were protected from on high.

Similarly, when the Jewish nation faced its greatest crisis through a decreed threat of annihilation in the days of King Xerxes, Queen Esther requested Mordecai to *'gather together all the Jews who are in Susa, and fast . . .'* (Esther 4:16). The outcome was that in spite of the overwhelming odds against them, the Jewish people were all spared and the enemy was destroyed in a sudden remarkable reversal of royal edicts.

If the principles and outcomes are timeless, then as we might expect, they will be confirmed today.

In 1991 Peru's much feared 'Shining Path' guerilla terrorist group, issued a death threat against that nation's National Director of 'Every Home Crusade', Philip Ortiz. 'Stop the work or pay the price with your life,' they said.

Through a method of tract distribution, Christian workers had been winning the battle for the hearts and minds of people who lived in the province which was a 'Shining Path' stronghold. Ortiz called for protective prayer cover and fasting for himself and his teams.

In the next two years, even though they travelled to the remotest villages on foot and known guerillas and drug traffickers were in their audiences, as they continued to preach and distribute their literature, no harm came to them from any source, including Peru's most feared guerilla group.[3]

Fifthly, we fast to seek revelation regarding the will of God.

Being heard in heaven is only half of the process for those of us who minister on earth. Obviously if the kingdom of God and the will of God is to be 'done on earth as it is in heaven' (Matthew 6:10), those of us who are instruments of its coming need to know the will of the Father and be willing to act accordingly.

The Bible records the well-known story of Daniel waiting before God for revelation. Daniel says that he *'turned to the Lord God and pleaded with him in prayer and petition, in fasting...'* (Daniel 9:3). Eventually the angel Gabriel was able to reach him and advise, *'Daniel, I have now come to give you insight and understanding'* (Daniel 9:22).

Stories such as this in the Bible do not guarantee that fasting must always result in such clear guidance. But it would seem that by fasting at least we place ourselves in a position where the Holy Spirit may have easier access to us.[4]

When the supply of foreign medicines failed to be available to a refuge for opium addicts, Pastor Hsi of China faced a major challenge. It was absolutely vital to have medicine to continue appropriate treatment of patients. With no other course of action available, Pastor Hsi desperately sought the Lord with prayer and fasting, as to what he might do.

As he continued to pray and fast, the Lord instructed him on which ingredients could be used and in what proportions. Having written out a prescription and compounded the various medicines, he hastened back to his refuge to administer the new mixture. It succeeded so well that it entirely changed aspects of early opium refuge work.

Whatever principles are called into operation, the general testimony is that prayer is intensified, spirituality is sensitised and ministry is more powerfully effective.

Derek Prince says that:

> 'Fasting deals with two great barriers to the Holy Spirit ... self-will ... and self-gratifying appetites of the body (Galatians 5:19) ... with these carnal barriers removed, the Holy Spirit can work unhindered in his fullness through our prayers ... fasting makes way for the Holy Spirit's omnipotence.[5]

However, we do need to remind ourselves that we do not fast out of self-centredness or to draw attention to ourselves. It occurs only within the context of prayer and worship 'unto the Lord.'

Jesus said that he was opposed to anything related to self-centredness with respect to prayer or fasting (Matthew 6:5–18). If we do it for selfish ends, forget it. It is not to be a means of getting something from God. It can never be reduced to formulas of exaggerated self-denial.

Fasting must be God initiated and God ordained (Isaiah 58). We are to be drawn by the Spirit, not dominated by the law (Galatians 5:18).

Fasting is not meant to impress others (Matthew 6:16–18; Luke 18:12). Nor is fasting a hunger strike to force God's hand to get our own way as politically inspired people sometimes like to do (Jeremiah 14:10–12). Fasting is not even meant to be a health kick. It is that which we do as a ministry unto the Lord.

For this reason God asked an earlier generation:

> *'When you fasted, was it really for me that you fasted?'*
> (Zechariah 7:5)

Was it self-initiated, self-ordained, self-promoted?

Whenever prayer and fasting are practised according to the

ways and will of the Lord, then we may expect extraordinary responses from him.

When Wayman Rogers, an American pastor, led his people in round the clock praying, he saw their church grow from 200 to 2,000. But when 200 people in the congregation began to fast every Thursday, the supernatural really broke through. He reports:

> 'A woman with cancer was healed. God delivered people from demon possession. Many people were healed by the miraculous power of God. For four and a half months we had a revival where 10,000 people came each week to our church. They argued over who was going to get the front seats. People were saved and healed and 4,600 people gave their hearts to God in that time. This was after the church had fasted and prayed for two years. The only problem we had was traffic jams ... Encourage your people to fast and pray.'[6]

And with that we can only agree.

Endnotes

1. This chapter is based on Chapter 2, *Praying the Price*, Stuart Robinson, Tonbridge, Kent: Sovereign World, 1994, 35–48.
2. Paul Y. Cho, *Prayer: Key to Revival*, 103.
3. *Every Home for Christ*, September 1993, 4.
4. Roland J. Hill, 'Fasting: A Discipline Ministers Need', *Ministry*, March 1990, 6–8.
5. Derek Prince, *Shaping History Through Prayer and Fasting*. Fort Lauderdale, Florida: Derek Prince Ministries, 1973, 86–87.
6. Wayman Rogers, 'Fasting', *Church Growth*, December, 1988.

Chapter 10

Praise Prayer

(Psalm 100:1–5)

Many years ago in the pioneering days of early missionary work in Thailand, a preacher wanted to go to a rather isolated animistic tribe. His friends tried to dissuade him because that particular tribe had a ferocious reputation. They said that he would be killed. But this preacher believed that the Holy Spirit wanted him to go. He would not be dissuaded.

When he reached the area which was the tribe's territory, he was suddenly surrounded by hostile men armed with spears. Not knowing what else to do, he started to pray and to praise God. He closed his eyes and commenced to sing a hymn 'All Hail the Power of Jesus Name'. When he finished, he opened his eyes and saw that every spear had been dropped. Tears were running down the cheeks of those warriors. They took him home and instead of killing him, gave him food and shelter. Later, they taught him their language and hundreds were converted.[1]

Praise in prayer and worship is something we often overlook, allowing ourselves to be overcome by our circumstances or by the culture in which our churches may be embedded. Certainly it is pleasing to God. Therefore we need to determine to do it.

1. Definition – To Glorify or Extol God

'To praise' means 'to express warm approval', 'to commend', 'to glorify' or 'to extol'. In the Old Testament, it meant to break out into a loud cry, especially that of joy. It conveyed the thought of making a noise. So great is the Lord that his people must draw attention to his glory. That was in part the reason behind God's great actions.

The Psalmist said:

> *'Let* (these things) *be written for a future generation,*
> *that a people not yet created may praise the Lord.'*
>
> (Psalm 102:18)

So we are encouraged to:

> *'Shout for joy to the Lord all the earth,*
> *burst into jubilant song with music...*
> *shout for joy before the Lord the King!'*   (Psalm 98:4, 6)

As God graciously revealed glimpses of his glory, it is natural for us to express our praise with intensity and volume.

2. Why Praise?

The apostle Paul said that:

> *'All things were created by Jesus Christ for Jesus Christ.'*
>
> (Colossians 1:16)

It is for his pleasure we exist.

Martin Luther once said:

> 'Since we receive everything from God, there is nothing that we can render to him but praise!'

Firstly, we are **created** to be praise for him. From the last book in the Bible we learn that:

> *'(He alone) is worthy to receive glory and honour and power, for he created all things and by his will they were created and have their being.'*   (Revelation 4:11)

Secondly, we are **encouraged** to praise him.

> *'Let us continually offer to God a sacrifice of praise.'*
> (Hebrews 13:15)

Thirdly, we are **commanded** to praise. The final Psalm commences with the command *'Praise the Lord.'* It concludes with:

> *'Let everything that has breath praise the Lord.*
> *Praise the Lord.'*   (Psalm 150)

Praise is our active response to what we know that God has done and is doing regardless of the appearance of things.

Paul said that we are to *'give thanks in all circumstances for this is God's will'* (1 Thessalonians 5:18). Note, we don't give thanks **for** all circumstances, but we must give thanks **in** all circumstances as a positive expression of our faith in God's goodness. This ensures that we do not live **under** the circumstances, but **over** the circumstances.

3. How?

How does praise occur? It commences from an attitude of the heart which releases an utterance from the mouth. What happens through the mouth is very important. The apostle John says that in his revelation he saw three evil spirits that came out of the mouth of the dragon, the beast and the false prophet (Revelation 16:13). The mouth can be a channel of great evil, or of blessing.

The Psalmist in part said:

> *'May the praise of God be in our mouths*
> *   and a double-edged sword in our hands,*
> *to inflict vengeance on the nations*
> *   and punishment on the peoples,*
> *to bind their kings with fetters . . .*
> *   This is the glory of all his saints.'*   (Psalm 149:6–9)

In view of what we know of the human history of Israel, and some of what we know of spiritual kingdoms, we may infer that these verses speak about more than physical kings. They also refer to principalities and powers which rule over nations.

Therefore, when we release praise to God from our mouths in prayer, we may wrap chains around satanic powers in the heavenlies and bind them so that they cannot function against us. In doing this, we are focusing on Christ. We are affirming that he already rules. We are demonstrating his victory in the midst of his enemies. We start to overcome with the word of testimony, to which the Bible refers (Revelation 12:11).

While praise is not to be regarded simply as a way to please God, to massage his heavenly ego or to gain favour with him so that we get what we want, it certainly brings results.

4. Results

(a) God's Presence is Increased

Firstly, God's presence is increased. The Psalmist said that:

> *'Yet you are enthroned as the Holy One;*
> *you are the praise of Israel.'* (Psalm 22:3)

To be *'enthroned'* means that he is present, that he takes his rightful place, that his presence will certainly be felt. Whenever there is a change in the king or the queen of a country, after some waiting, the monarch is enthroned. Everybody becomes very much aware of it. There is a new king on the throne.

With God's enthronement, he steps out of his mystery into our history and we move from our history into his mystery. Then we discover secondly that:

(b) Darkness is Dismissed

Praise always destroys an atmosphere of sickness, defeat, discouragement and futility. It cleanses our surroundings.

In a newspaper cartoon I read recently, a wife greets her husband who staggers through the door at the end of the day. Concerned about air pollution she asks, 'How's the quality of the air out there?'

He replies:

'It's putrid. It's frightening. It's full of toxic particles and terrible smells. I'm choking. There are particles of malice, particles of fear, particles of smashed hope, broken trust, shattered values. I feel sick.

There is the smell of resentment, the smell of frustration, the smell of envy, the rotten stench of callous disregard, I can't breathe.

There are particles of bitterness, particles of bad faith, particles of modern madness. I'm suffocating. I can't live properly.'

And then he shouts, 'I want some good atmosphere!'

Finally, the wife replies, 'Just hold on – I'll get the dog.'

Although that cartoon may well have been describing the physical atmosphere of Calcutta, Bangkok or Melbourne, I don't know that getting the dog would have helped. But in the spiritual sense moving to praise certainly does. It almost seems as if Satan and his representatives are in some way allergic to praise. They seem to become paralysed, bound or banished when in prayer we praise.

Continuous praise may give continuous victory. Why? Because God is enthroned and presences himself in our praise. Satan and his demons fear his presence.

> '*From the lips of children and infants you have ordained praise . . .*
> *to silence the foe and the avenger.*' (Psalm 8:2)

Our supreme foe or enemy, is he who accuses us day and night. That is exactly what Satan does continuously before the throne of God (Revelation 12:10). He is silenced when we release praise!

Martin Luther, who was very aware of often being opposed by demonic forces, once wrote:

'When I cannot pray, I always sing. Singing spikes the devil.'[2]

If things seem unendingly hopeless, start praising God and feel Satan's hosts flee.

The third result of praise is that praise changes us.

(c) *Praise Changes Us*

As we start to praise God, we change our focus from our fears and doubts on to God's presence and power. We move from concentrating on the battle to ' anticipating the victory. We move from the complexity of the problem to the adequacy of God's resources, from the urgency of our needs to the power of the Lord to meet those needs. The fog of our understanding starts to clear so that we can see things more from God's perspective as we relinquish preoccupation with ourselves and direct our attention toward God.

The Psalmist said:

'When I am afraid,
   I will trust in you.
In God, whose word I praise,
   in God I trust; I will not be afraid.'   (Psalm 56:3–4)

The fourth result is that our faith increases.

(d) *Faith Increases*

As we concentrate on God, the mountain we may be facing starts to grow smaller in the light of God's greatness. King David once told how when he was in great difficulty he sought God. He took his eyes off himself and his circumstances and started to praise God. Then God solved his problems (Psalm 34:4–7).

Let's look at some examples of how this works out in practical living.

5. Examples

(a) *King Jehoshaphat* (2 Chronicles 20:1–30)

King Jehoshaphat received news that a large army was invading his kingdom from the east. Recognising that Jehoshaphat had totally inadequate military resources to withstand such an attack, he proclaimed a fast throughout Judah. Then, through one of the Levites, a prophetic word was received from God which gave encouragement, assurance and direction. This resulted in spontaneous worship, prayer and praise amongst the people.

Jehoshaphat quickly organised continuing praise to lead his people into battle. Singers preceded his small army with the result that the overwhelming enemy turned in chaos and destroyed themselves. By use of the weapons of fasting, prayer, gifts, worship and especially praise, there resulted a remarkable demonstration of how battles are fought in the spiritual realm, which effect the physical realm.

(b) *Paul and Silas* (Acts 16:16–28)

Acts records the story of how Paul and Silas delivered a slave girl from an evil spirit. This stirred up the principalities and powers over the city of Philippi so that the citizens irrationally turned on Paul and Silas as a result of that healing. They beat them and threw them into goal.

However, Paul and Silas kept their heads and their hearts together and instead of feeling sorry for themselves, 'they prayed and sang hymns to God,' which resulted in an earthquake and everyone's chains being loosed! Prayer and praise released God's ministering angels to intervene in the circumstances.

(c) *China*

At the turn of this century, during what was known as the 'Boxer Uprising' in China, Reverend Glover and his family were fleeing from death. Finally Mrs Glover collapsed on the ground. She was utterly exhausted, sick and unable to move any further. Hunger, thirst and heat had also defeated her.

Then a lady by the name of Miss Gates, one of their party, knelt down beside her and poured forth passage after passage, promise after promise from the Scriptures, exalting the Lord's name, declaring his faithfulness and his unchanging love towards them.

Mr Glover later wrote:

'Instantly the darkness was passed and light was shining again. My wife, who seemed to be dying, was suddenly revived. She sat up with restored vigour which amazed me. Through every future trial she simply went on from strength to strength.'[3]

A hymn writer expressed the process like this:

'How sweet the name of Jesus sounds
in a believers ear.
It soothes his sorrows, heals his wounds,
and drives away his fear.'

In an attempt to destroy his sanity Richard Wurmbrand had been kept in solitary confinement and tortured for three years in Communist prisons in Rumania. When he reached the end of his ability to endure, he started to speak aloud Scriptures of promise, of God's faithfulness and majesty, of his greatness and everlasting love. Wurmbrand started to pray and to praise God. 'Then,' he said, 'my prison cell started to radiate with joy and the presence of God who was being enthroned in that dark place.'

English evangelist David Watson wrote of how agnostics and atheists submitted to God, of how people were healed of multiple sclerosis and cancer, of how relationships were restored, faith and hope were renewed, of people being dramatically changed in the presence of God's people when they were caught up in worship, prayer and praise.[4]

6. Action

There are at least two things we need to do.

Firstly, we need to decide to put on a garment of praise instead of a Spirit of despair (Isaiah 61:3). We have been offered a garment, but it is we, by an act of our will, who need to put it on. When we do that, God responds.

A battle is won by decisions which are made in a moment. But the results are lived out in subsequent years. We need to decide again to be a praying, praising people. This will revolutionise our lives and change the way in which we see and do things.

Secondly, we need to declare, 'God, I believe you are whom you claim to be, in all of your fullness and your faithfulness.'

We need to remind ourselves that God has not changed. Certainly Jesus will never change (Hebrews 13:8). We need to agree with that we also *'will forget not all his benefits'* (Psalm 103:2).

With King David we will declare:

> *'I will praise the Lord, who counsels me . . .*
> *Because he is at my right hand,*
> *I will not be shaken.'*   (Psalm 16:7–8)

There is no substitute for praise. It honours God. It brings joy to the angels. It strikes terror in every evil spirit. It clears the atmosphere. It washes our spirit. It increases our faith and clothes us with God's presence and power.

> *'Praise the Lord, O my soul;*
> *all my inmost being, praise his holy name.'*
>   (Psalm 103:1)

> *'Glorify the Lord with me;*
> *let us exalt his name together.'*   (Psalm 34:3)

> *'Shout for joy to the Lord, all the earth,*
> *Worship the Lord with gladness;*
> *come before him with joyful songs.*
> *Know that the Lord is God.*
> *It is he who made us, and we are his;*
> *we are his people, the sheep of his pasture.*

*Enter his gates with thanksgiving
and his courts with praise;
give thanks to him and praise his name.
For the Lord is good and his love endures forever;
his faithfulness continues through all generations.'*

(Psalm 100:1–5)

From a position of strength we then begin to pray in the 'harvest'.

Endnotes

1. Ira Sankey, *My Life and Sacred Songs*, 1906.
2. Wesley L. Duewel, *Touch the World Through Prayer*. Grand Rapids, Michigan: Francis Ashbury Press, 1986, 142.
3. Derek Prince, *Created to Praise*. London: Hodder & Stoughton, 1981, pp. 39ff.
4. David Watson, *Fear No Evil*. London: Hodder & Stoughton, 1984, 61.

Chapter 11

Prayer and the Harvest

(Matthew 9:35–10:1)

Eric Moore was the Project Coordinator for new heavy equipment which was being installed at Christian radio station HCJB, which operates from Quito in Ecuador.

After a busy day of conferring with colleagues, checking the progress of various aspects of the latest project, taking important phone calls and detailing work to contractors for the next day, Eric headed out at dusk on to the road for the 30 kilometre drive back to his home in Pifo.

The road was winding and wind-blown as it slithered over the high-altitude Andes Mountains. Little traffic was usually encountered at this time of the evening. Eric knew every dip and turn, every pot-hole and wash-out that there was on that road. But suddenly his vehicle lurched and in the next instant Eric found himself off the road and rolling down the mountain side. When his vehicle finally stopped, Eric's leg was firmly pinned underneath it. In the darkness he feared the worst – fire.

Minutes passed. As Eric lay trapped there, thoughts raced through his mind. 'How much blood am I losing? Will anyone ever find me down here?' He began to pray. 'Lord, help me!'

Around the other side of the world at the church in Eric's home town in Ireland, people were meeting in a weekly Bible study group. Suddenly, one of the members was prompted to say, 'I believe we should stop and pray for the Moores in Ecuador.'

Immediately the meeting was halted and they engaged in a time of very earnest prayer for the Moore family, asking the Lord to meet whatever the need was right at that time.

Back in Ecuador a passing motorist stopped to investigate what seemed to be some object down the slope. Eric was found and rescued. Later it was discovered that as they prayed back in Ireland, at that very moment God heard and answered.

God's people had responded to the prompting of the Holy Spirit and God had honoured their prayers.

Repeatedly missionaries in far-off places are dependent for their very lives on those who have committed themselves to pray. But the question which arises from time to time in almost every missionary's mind is, of those who have made such a commitment, how many actually follow through on it?

I well remember one of my first experiences in a life-threatening situation in Asia. I had been quietly riding along the road at dusk on a bicycle, when suddenly two men swooped in behind me on their bikes to try to steal what I had behind me on my carrier. A scuffle ensued. I managed to escape, but they caught up with me. A crowd gathered. It could have been a nasty scene.

These men wanted to take me over into a paddock at the side of the road to deal with me permanently with the knives they carried. In the midst of the shouting, confusion and danger, there came a question into my mind: 'I wonder who at home is praying for me now?'

I remember many times when I would be out searching for food to try to find something, some fruit, some fish, some rice, something of anything to take home for my young family, when there was danger and violence in the country-side. And I would wonder at such times, 'Who is praying for us now?'

I remember when my wife Margaret and daughter Krystal were alone and men came with guns. Their lives were in jeopardy. Again the question came, 'Who is praying for us now?'

I remember working for days and nights on end in floods and famine conditions where we would measure success or failure rates in terms of the number of corpses which would be found at the railway station, on the river banks or at other places each day. As we worked, cut off from communication, I would ask myself, 'Who is praying for us now?'

I remember the many times armoured tanks were stuttering their machine guns and blasting their cannons outside our doors, rifle fire was slamming here and there, planes were rocketing overhead, and I would ask myself, 'Who is praying for us now?'

I remember as we were baptising new believers, converts from a traditionally hostile non-Christian religious community, in which there was an element of danger attached to such activity, where lives could literally be on the line. I would ask myself the question, 'Who is praying for us now?'

As any missionary who travels around speaking with Christian groups knows full well, literally thousands of people after those deputation meetings meet the speaker at the door of various churches and halls, shake that person's hand and frequently say, 'Thank you, brother. Thank you, sister. We'll keep in touch. We'll pray for you.' But one never hears from them ever again.

The commitment to pray on behalf of the missionary work force, is a special and serious obligation. In fact without it, there will be few if any missionaries going forth at all. And if they do, without prayer backing, success if any will be very limited.

According to Jesus, prayer has a very specific role to play (Matthew 9:35–10:1).

Jesus had been very active in ministry, teaching, preaching and healing. Then,

> *'When he saw the crowds he had compassion on them, because they were harassed and helpless, like sheep without a shepherd.'*
> (Matthew 9:36)

132

They seemed lost. They didn't know where to go or what to do. They were hungry. They had no one to help them. No one to feed them. Physically and spiritually that is still the situation in many countries today.

I have often lived and worked in situations where people, to get some sort of food have queued in their thousands, hoped in their hundreds, fought, fainted and died right on our door steps. Even today and every day about 10,000 people are going to die of starvation. There is an enormous physical need not being met in the world.

And the spiritual need is just as great.

I have been in situations where representatives of thousands have been sent to me to enquire about Jesus Christ. Because of commitments elsewhere I couldn't go myself and nor did I have anyone else to send in my place.

I cannot begin to convey what it feels like to be in that situation and to live with the memory of those years. I knew that because I had no resources to offer, and nothing more to give myself, that I was possibly denying people who wanted to know the Way, entrance into the kingdom of God.

In the first group of new believers who were baptised in the area where we were working, there was a man who for 10 years had been searching for the truth. He had heard about Jesus Christ. He had gone hither and yon across the land seeking anyone who would sit down and talk with him to tell him the truth about Jesus. But there was no one.

Another man obtained a Christian tract. For five years he used to keep it on a high shelf in his home. He used to take it down occasionally to re-read it, always hoping that one day he would meet someone who could help him understand more about this Jesus.

There have been times which I can never forget, when outside of the doors and the windows of the various places we called 'home', there were endless crowds knocking on the doors, ringing the bell, tapping on the windows, all desperate for help, wanting teaching, conversation – anything. Unable to cope, I went inside, locked and bolted the doors and wept with frustration and grief at not being able to meet those needs, to answer those calls, to teach enquirers or to feed the hungry ones.

The physical and spiritual hunger which exists in so many countries of the world is still enormous. Only a fraction of God's lost sheep ever find the way back to him because they still have no shepherd to guide them.

'Jesus said to his disciples, "The harvest is plentiful, but the workers are few."' (Matthew 9:37)

In some difficult access countries, Bible correspondence schools are set up and hundreds of thousands enrol with little advertising. In just one middle-eastern city, a single tiny advertisement for a Bible study course resulted in 20,000 responses.

In other countries Bible distributors sell hundreds of thousands of units per month. They have been unable to keep up with the demand.

A man wandered into the office of a Christian leader in the capital city of a certain country. He had come from a rather inhospitable area in that land. Because it was somewhat of a sanctuary for rebels and therefore a hot spot of military conflict and police action, certainly no foreigners were ever allowed into that area. Movement was restricted. No missionaries had ever been there.

When the Christian leader asked him who he was and what he wanted, he gave his name and said, 'I represent the such and such church.' To which the Christian leader replied, 'The what church?'

Again the newcomer told the leader the name of it.

The Christian leader replied, 'Tell me more about this church.'

So the man told his story of how a few years previously when he was ill he came from where his people lived and went for treatment to a Christian hospital where he heard about Jesus Christ. He was one of the few people in his area that knew how to read and write. So he took a Bible, went back home, read it, believed it, and started to preach about this Jesus mentioned in this Bible. As he stood before the capital city leader he said, 'Within a few years time there were 4,000 new believers. Within eight years that had grown to 12,000 believers.' Just a few years ago they received their first edition of an officially translated Bible into their own language. Sometimes God does amazing things almost without any human help!

Jesus said:

> *'The harvest is plentiful, but the workers are few.'*
> (Matthew 9:37).

In place after place where workers are so few then the tragic result of that is seen in the compelling logic of the apostle Paul when he said:

> *'How then can they call upon the one they have not believed in? And how can they believe in the one of whom they have not heard? And how can they hear without someone preaching to them? And how can they preach unless they are sent?'*
> (Romans 10:14)

- If no one is sent, then no one preaches.
- If no one preaches, then they do not hear.
- If they do not hear, then they cannot believe.
- If they cannot believe, then...?

In the wake of a giant tidal wave, in shimmering sunshine and deathly silence I once wandered through a flattened deserted area with bloated bodies clogging canals, protruding from embankments or stuck up trees. There was nothing left living other than crows and vultures gorging on fetid flesh.

500,000 people had been killed in one night alone. To the best of our knowledge, because of the remote area in which they lived, no one had ever told them about Jesus, because the labourers were too few.

I remember standing alone in the smouldering ruins of villages which had been razed with flame throwers the night before. In this area in nine months, three million were killed and ten million fled to refugee camps. As far as we know, so very few of them would ever have heard the good news of Jesus Christ, because the labourers were too few.

I remember being in another country watching bodies swirl down flooded rivers thinking again, they never heard. They never heard. They never heard. There was no one to tell them. The workers were too few. 'Lord, for how long must this continue?'

In the disaster areas of this world how long must masses tumble into the abyss of ultimate disaster dying into an eternity without ever having a chance of encountering the living Lord?

In the light of this situation, what is our responsibility? Jesus said:

> *'The harvest is plentiful, but the workers are few. Ask (pray), the Lord of harvest, therefore, to send out workers into his harvest field.'*

'To ask' (or 'to pray') is a verb in the imperative mood. It is a command. Jesus said the anticipated result of obedience to this command is that workers will be 'sent out' (Matthew 9:38). The word used for 'sending out' is exactly the same as that used in the very next verse for 'driving out' evil spirits (Matthew 10:1).

Prayer creates the conditions in which the Holy Spirit can work. It seems that what is required is an element of forceful action on the part of the Holy Spirit to break into, to break forth, to shake out those labourers that he wants to thrust out of our churches into vastly more needy areas.

'Pray therefore,' Jesus says.

Pray!

- He does not say to form a committee to review the matter.
- He does not say to pack and send food parcels.
- He does not say to send birthday and Christmas cards.
- He does not say to collect used clothing for the poor.
- He does not even say to hold a missionary convention, or to give money as much as these practical expressions of love and concern are necessary and appreciated.

The command for the urgent need of this time is to pray.
For in no other way will workers be thrust forth. Unless we do
that, all we have is scaffolding without a building.

A South Asian friend of mine on his first visit to Korea,
preached in a Korean church which at that time had a
membership of many tens of thousands. It has since grown
much larger. He was amazed at this vast and repeated
gathering of Christian believers.

He asked the senior pastor of that church what was the
secret of all that was happening? The pastor took him to a
large room at the back of the church. He opened the door to
find that it was crowded with people who were praying.
Twenty four hours a day prayer issued forth from that room.
The pastor said, 'There is the secret of what has happened in
this church, and for what is happening in our nation.'

When the apostle Paul concluded his teaching on spiritual
warfare, he said:

> *'Pray in the Spirit on all occasions, with all kinds of prayer
> and requests. With this in mind, be alert and always keep on
> praying...'* (Ephesians 6:18)

'Pray therefore,' Jesus said.

When it comes to praying and identifying labourers for the
harvest, this should not necessarily be allowed to depend
exclusively upon young people's personal response. It is a
responsibility of the whole church.

Of the early church we read:

> *'While they were worshipping the Lord and fasting, the Holy
> Spirit said, "Set apart for me Barnabas and Saul for the work
> to which I have called them." So after they had fasted and
> prayed, they placed their hands on them and sent them off.'*
> (Acts 13:2–3)

And so the mission to the Gentiles commenced. God spoke
to the leaders of the church identifying whom he wanted and
the leaders acted in response to that. They did not sit back
and wait for some young people to wrestle on their own with

a call from God and come forward. The leadership was so in touch with God as to know what God was saying.

In various ways in previous days, I might never have recognised my own call to Christian ministry had it not been for two senior Christians in the church in which I was a member. They came to me and said, 'Stuart, we believe you have the gifts for the ministry.'

I might not have ever become a missionary to a Third World country had it not been for another friend who persistently came to me saying, 'Stuart, I believe God wants you for Asia.'

I would not have accepted or even known of a call to my current position had it not been for people who were senior in the faith coming to me saying, 'Stuart, we believe that God is calling you to that ministry.'

When it comes to identifying the workers, don't leave it necessarily up to the young people to struggle on their own.

'Ask the Lord of the harvest,' Jesus said.

What an extraordinary context. There was Jesus surrounded by masses of well meaning, busy, sincere, religious people. But he says, there were few labourers.

Amongst God's people in that day there were ecclesiastical technocrats. There were plenty of theologians from fundamentalists to liberals. They had their 'conventions'. They had their committees to review and plan strategy. They had their deeper life enthusiasts, whole monasteries full of them. They had their crusading evangelistic zealots. They had their Scripture colleges, their schools and their highly qualified teachers. They had plenty of nice buildings in which to meet for worship. But in terms of meeting the spiritual needs of the day, they were destitute.

So concerned were they about their tradition and their theology, their doctrine and practice, as to not even notice the condition of the sheep. The whole fabric of their religious structure and their careful attention to the maintenance of the status quo, served only to entomb them away from the life of God and what he wanted to do. And as the Lord looks out over the Christian religious scene today, I wonder what he sees which could be different.

He certainly sees vast crowds and has compassion on them, because they also are often harassed and helpless like sheep without a shepherd. Therefore he still says:

> *'The harvest is plentiful, but the workers are few. Ask the Lord of the harvest, therefore, to send out workers into his harvest field.'*

And then he calls his twelve disciples to him and gives them authority to drive out evil spirits, to cure every kind of disease and sickness, to get on to multiply the ministry (Matthew 10:1) Later, in that same Gospel of Matthew, again he says to his disciples:

> *'... Go and make disciples of all nations ... teaching them to obey everything I have commanded you.'*
>
> (Matthew 28:19–20)

Still later on he encouraged them to wait in Jerusalem. He said:

> *'You will receive power when the Holy Spirit comes on you, and you will be my witnesses in Jerusalem, and in all Judea, Samaria, and to the ends of the earth.'* (Acts 1:8)

Acts 2 is the record of how that power was received.

Acts 3 records how it started to be released.

Luke and Acts are the record of all that Jesus began to do. And he wants to do these same things today.

Whether that continues to happen or not depends on how serious we are in obeying our Lord in fulfilling a commission and a commandment which was given, to be constantly asking the Lord of the harvest to thrust forth labourers into his harvest.

If we do not, what may result?

I remember hearing of one missionary who, when he was called, agreed to go forth to another country if his church would hold the ropes and intercede on his behalf. Two years later with his wife and child both dead, he returned a broken man. Unnoticed, he slipped into the back seat of the prayer meeting in his church.

At the end of the meeting he rose and said, 'I am your missionary whom you sent forth. My wife and child lie buried in Africa and I am sick with disease. I listened to your prayer to see if you had kept your promise, but in vain. You failed to hold the ropes.'

But if we do pray, then what happens?

In Chapter 8 I referred to a call for a million intercessors and some of what has happened since. That 1992 challenge was at the instigation of Dr C. Peter Wagner and the AD 2000 Prayer Track. It was for a million intercessors to pray for the 62 countries which have proved more difficult to reach than others (that is the 10/40 window – 10°–40° north of the equator). In fact 20 million joined in praying. In October 1995 the process was repeated. But this time 36.7 million intercessors joined in.

Additional reported macro results:

- Greater freedom for preaching the Gospel.
- Demonic powers weakened.
- Key national leaders experiencing dreams and visions of Jesus.
- An increase in the miraculous.
- Church populations in some countries growing at double the rate of national population growth.
- 25 million converts in the last four years in one country,[1] and
- 'In the last few years the number of missionaries has increased from a mere 1,000 to over 2,000 among the 1.1 billion Muslims.'[2]

Regardless of age, understanding, maturity in the faith or whatever, the command is that we are to, 'Pray to the Lord of the harvest.' We are required, not just to send out workers but to stand by them and to be praying continually for them. We need to make a commitment to do that alone in our homes and to come together to do likewise as it was from the beginning of the church, until the commission of going to all the people of the world is complete.

And for some of us, we need to be ready to be the Lord's answer to our own prayers. And we may well be if our attitude is right.

Endnotes

1. 'Praying Through the Window 111', *The Unreached Peoples*. The Christian Information Network, Colorado Springs, USA: nd.
2. Keith Greig, *'30 Days Muslim Prayer Focus'*, Newsletter. Buderim, Queensland, Australia: August 12, 1997.

Chapter 12

Attitudes

(Genesis 28:20; Psalm 116:1 &
Habakkuk 3:17)

Jacob had deceived his father Isaac and had got a blessing from him which had been meant for his older brother Esau. At this stage in his life, Jacob was hardly on intimate personal terms with God. When his father Isaac questioned him, Jacob replied, *'The Lord your God gave me success'* (Genesis 27:20).

Jacob knew about God from his father, Isaac. But his father's God was not yet his God. As a result of the stolen blessing, Jacob had to flee from the anger of his brother Esau.

During his flight Jacob lay down to rest for the night and had a dream. In the dream, the Lord promised him that he would give to him and to his descendants multiplied blessings.

> *'All peoples on earth will be blessed through you and your offspring. I am with you and will watch over you wherever you go, and I will bring you back to this land. I will not leave you until I have done what I have promised you. When Jacob awoke from his sleep, he thought, "Surely the Lord is in this place, and I was not aware of it." He was afraid and said, "How awesome is this place! This is none other than the house of God; this is the gate of heaven."'*

(Genesis 28:14–17)

How sad it is that often we are just like Jacob. We have an encounter with God and we are unaware of it until after the event. So like him we say, *'Surely the Lord is in this place, and I was not aware of it.'*

As a result of this encounter Jacob then utters an extraordinary prayer in the form of a vow.

1. 'If'

> *'If God will be with **me** and will watch over **me** on this journey I am taking and will give **me** food to eat and clothes to wear so that I return safely to **my** father's house, then the Lord will be **my** God and this stone that I have set up as a pillar will be God's house, and of all that you give **me** I will give you a tenth.'*
> (Genesis 28:20–22)

Notice Jacob's attitude. He attempts in his immature knowledge of God, to bargain with the Almighty. 'If you O Lord, will do this and this and this and this for me, if you will make me well off and rich and safe, then of all that you give to me, I will give you a tenth.' Big deal!

I wonder how often God hears such prayers from us.

During my childhood, one day I was swinging on the front gate at our home. My father had repeatedly warned me never to swing on that gate. If I did it might not be good for my health.

As I swung on the gate that day, it suddenly groaned, pulled from its post and sank slowly to the ground. In distress and despair I ran up the drive to our home. I flung myself down on the stairs and begged and pleaded with God to fix that gate before my father returned home from work. I prayed, 'O Lord if you will fix that gate, I promise that I will be a good boy for ever after.'

God seemed to forget my prayer. But my father did not forget his promise and it was not good for my health.

In my final year of high school, when I did a pre-final exam test and got only 14% for chemistry, again I begged and pleaded with God, 'Lord, if only you will get me through the final exam, I promise you that I will be ever such a good, disciplined student in the future. I will never leave my study to the last weeks before exams, ever again.'

God didn't seem to hear that prayer and neither did I keep my part of the bargain.

On another occasion when my father's seafood processing businesses were in great financial difficulty, like many other desperate businessmen, suddenly he seemed to turn to God. He prayed, 'Lord, if you get me out of this financial mess I promise you that I will acknowledge you and I will even go to church and be generous toward your work.' On that particular occasion, the Lord did not seem to answer that prayer either. My father certainly never kept his part of the commitment.

How many times have others of us in desperation prayed 'Lord, if only you will heal my sick child; if only you will get me a job; if only you will save my husband; if only you will help me to get to know that beautiful girl who could be my future wife; if only you will bring rain for good harvest; if only you would stop the rain so we don't have floods . . .'

How often in our immaturity do we dare to propose a bargain with God Almighty? The extraordinary thing is that he is prepared even to listen to us when our attitudes are so infantile and our motives are so self-centred.

In Jacob's case, God actually accepted what Jacob offered. However, we need to be careful. If we would thus pray, remember this, that when we make such commitments God may take us seriously.

Later God said to Jacob:

> *'I am the God of Bethel, where you anointed a pillar and where you made a vow to me.'*　　　　(Genesis 31:13)

God was reminding Jacob of what he had said and the contract he had proposed. God **remembers** even when we might rather forget.

Amazingly God also **accepts**. Later Jacob prayed and said:

> *'I am unworthy of all the kindness and faithfulness you
> (O Lord) have shown your servant. I had only my staff when
> I crossed this Jordan, but now I have become two groups.'*
>
> (Genesis 32:10)

So God had prospered Jacob according his request. God
accepted Jacob's proposal.

But we need to be aware that not only does God remember
and accept, he also holds us **accountable**.

> *'Then God said to Jacob, "Go up to Bethel and settle there,
> and build an altar there to God, who appeared to you when
> you were fleeing from your brother Esau."'*   (Genesis 35:1)

Jacob had said that if God did so much for him, so that he
could return safely to his father's house, then the Lord would
be his God. God was now calling in the contract and
demanding to be treated as God. He **remembers**, he **accepts**
and he holds us **accountable**.

Even such a prayer as **'If'** is amazingly heard and sometimes accepted by God.

However, when we pray there is a somewhat better
attitude.

2. 'Because'

In Psalm 116 David is looking back on his life. As he
contemplates all that has happened he says:

> *'I love the Lord, because he heard my voice;*
>   *he heard my cry for mercy.*
> *Because he turned his ear to me,*
>   *I will call on him as long as I live.'*   (Psalm 116:1)

Then he goes on reminiscing. He refers to the *'cords of death
entangling him,'* the *'anguish of the grave'* and how he was
'almost overcome by trouble and sorrow' (Psalm 116:3).

Later he talks about *'death and tears and stumbling'* (v. 8),
about being *'greatly afflicted'* (v.10). Coming through to the
other side of his life, he realises that he needs to make a fresh

commitment and so he says, *'I will fulfil my vows to the Lord, in the presence of his people'* (v. 14). *'O Lord, truly I am your servant; ... You have freed me from my chains'* (v. 16). *'I will sacrifice a thank offering to you and call on the name of the Lord'* (v. 17). *'I will fulfil my vows to the Lord in the presence of all his people ...'* (v. 18). *'Praise the Lord'* (v. 19).

I'm sure that each of us as we look back over our lives, can find many events which in thankfulness can lift us from an attitude of bargaining with God in prayer, to where we find David now.

When I was working in Asia during one of its many wars, millions were being killed as more millions were fleeing across borders of neighbouring countries into refugee camps. Day after day I went out trying to see if any friends were still alive, trying to bring encouragement and comfort to whomever. All the roads were blocked. Communications were out. One day I took my bicycle and said to my wife that I was going to try to find a little food and visit some people in a far off place.

I hadn't been gone long when Margaret received word from the local post office, that I had been shot and killed. In case she didn't believe them, they phoned again later to re-emphasise that I had been killed. Still they felt that she didn't understand and so they sent a delegation of people out to our home where she was now living alone on the edge of a town.

After the men left, Margaret took our only child Krystal, who was just a young girl and explained to her that perhaps she was now without a father and that they were completely cut off and alone in the midst of a war.

Yes, it's true that sometimes I was shot at. It's true that the days were very dangerous. Yes, we did lose everything. But, on that particular day obviously I wasn't killed.

I think of those events and how we also eventually became refugees and of how the Lord later resupplied all of our needs exactly according to that which was lost. And I can say, 'I love the Lord, **because** he heard my voice, to protect my family.'

On another occasion when our daughter was dying and we had no access to medical help. The local doctor's assistant had advised us to see if the veterinary surgeon could help. All we could do was to lay our hands upon our daughter, thank the Lord for the gift she had been to us and commend her back to him, while at the same time asking him mercifully to heal her. She could have died within hours, but instead as another woman died metres away on the side of the road, for our daughter things were turned around and she lived.

Today she and her husband are parents of their own daughter.

'I love the Lord, **because** he heard my voice.'

On another occasion when we were living alone in a remote place and my wife lost a baby. There was nothing we could do about it other than to ask God to help in some way. Within hours a British lady gynaecologist came into our home. It had never happened before or since. But she just 'happened' to land at a nearby airport and felt 'nudged' to come and see us. She was able to tend expertly to my wife's needs.

'I love the Lord, **because** he heard my voice.'

Some years later Margaret was in a Red Cross hospital. She had been losing blood for days on end. She was drifting in and out of consciousness. We didn't know what to do. Suddenly two friends turned up and there in a loud voice started to pray. I was so embarrassed I wanted to hide under the bed. The doctor had already told us that the baby in Margaret was dead and all that was needed was a clean out operation. But these two friends prayed vigorously, and then advised me all would be well.

Margaret's bleeding stopped without medication, for there was none available. The result, against all odds was that the child lived and today he is a very healthy young man. A miracle baby.

'I love the Lord, **because** he heard my voice.'

In another tough situation when my family and another family were in the midst of a bombing raid. Overhead planes were diving to see if they could destroy vehicles left by 'freedom fighters' outside our home. The noise of the rockets falling around us was overwhelming. In a moment of silence I suggested to those gathered in our home, that we sing a well known chorus, 'When we all get to heaven...' One of my colleagues suggested perhaps it ought to be, 'If we all get to heaven...' Thereupon ensued a wonderful theological argument about the certainty of salvation. We had a great laugh in the midst of such chaos.

'I love the Lord, **because** he heard my voice.'

There are so many events which have occurred in my life when I and my family have been threatened. There have been so many trials, when it seemed as if even all believers were mostly against us as God was attempting to do new things through us in ministry in this country or in that. God has always come through. Truly I can say,

'I love the Lord, **because** he has heard my voice.'

Through these experiences we have learned to thank God for the blackest times, because it is on such occasions there is opportunity for his glory to shine brightest.

Surely it is possible, whether we have been walking with the Lord for little or long, that we no longer need to pray like Jacob 'If', but rather with David say, 'Because'.

3. 'Although'

There is however an even better attitude that we can bring to our relationship with God. We find it at the end of the book of Habakkuk (Habakkuk 3:17). The background is that the prophet Habakkuk lived in days of great anxiety and personal distress. Like many counterparts before and since he complained to God about the situation in which he found himself.

> *'How long, O Lord, must I call for help,*
> *but you do not listen?*
> *Or cry out to you, "Violence!"*
> *but you do not save?*

> *Why do you make me look at injustice?*
>   *Why do you tolerate wrong?*
> *Destruction and violence are before me;*
>   *there is strife, and conflict abounds.*
> *Therefore the law is paralysed,*
>   *and justice never prevails.*
> *The wicked hem in the righteous,*
>   *so that justice is perverted.'*
>
> (Habakkuk 1:1–4)

'Have you gone to sleep up there God? Have you gone on holidays? Are you deaf? Can't you hear me? Are you blind? Can't you see what's happening? How long are you going to put up with this? Come on, do something!' Sound familiar?

Against his complaint the Lord gives an extraordinary answer, in part of which he says:

> *'Look at the nations and watch –*
>   *and be utterly amazed.*
> *For I am going to do something in your days*
>   *that you would not believe,*
>   *even if you were told.*
> *I am raising up the Babylonians . . .'*
>
> (Habakkuk 1:5–6)

The concept was so preposterous and too frightening even to contemplate. The Babylonians were savage military people. And although God had spoken this extraordinary word, it would seem that Habakkuk couldn't even comprehend it. Instead he blithely continues on with his complaint and then says:

> *'You cannot tolerate wrong;*
>   *you cannot tolerate wrong.*
> *Why then do you tolerate the treacherous?*
>   *Why are you silent when the wicked*
>   *swallow up those more righteous than themselves?'*
>
> (Habakkuk 1:13)

If ever you feel like that, remember that although we must settle our accounts, especially with the Taxation Department by the end of every financial year, God is not so obliged.

At the end of his complaint Habakkuk petulantly declares:

> *'I will stand at my watch*
> *and station myself on the ramparts;*
> *I will look to see what he will say to me,*
> *and what answer I am to give to this complaint.'*
>
> (Habakkuk 2:1)

'There Lord, I've had my say. Now, what are you going to say to me?'

The answer comes quickly. The Lord gives him a revelation and advises him to wait for an appointed time:

> *'Though it linger, wait for it;*
> *it will certainly come and will not delay.'*
>
> (Habakkuk 2:3)

How we need to learn that *'He to whom a thousand years is as a day'* (Psalm 90:4 and 2 Peter 3:8) is seldom in the same hurry that we demand of him. How often do we impatiently pray a whole shopping list of requests and then say to the Lord, 'Do it now.'

We need the reminder:

> *'Do not throw away your confidence; it will be richly rewarded. You have need to persevere so that when you have done the work of God, you will receive what he has promised.'*
>
> (Hebrews 10:35)

Unfortunately, in our world we are pre-conditioned to instantaneous gratification.

> 'We are the microwave generation and we just can't wait for the "Ping!" We want to be told that . . . a problemless tomorrow is just a visualisation away. We want to be told that a workshop can eradicate all those yucky emotions in the time it takes a TV washing powder to get out the beetroot stain on a before-and-after-shirt.
>
> We want to believe that we can control every single detail of our reality and that the universe waits for us to snap our fingers so it can do our bidding.'[1]

But God will neither be hurried nor controlled by the immediacy of our urgent demands. He reminds Habakkuk that, '... *the righteous will live by faith*' (Habakkuk 2:4).

We are also told that:

> '*Faith is being sure of what we hope for and certain of what we do not see.*' (Hebrews 11:1)

> '*And without faith it is impossible to please God.*' (Hebrews 11:6)

This is the way he requires us to live. Faith is spelt 'R-I-S-K'. Faith is walking in the midst of miracles always on the edge of disaster. And to what might we look forward? That '*the earth will be filled with the knowledge of the glory of the Lord, as the waters cover the sea*' (Habakkuk 2:14) is our ultimate expectation.

The tremendous growth that we are seeing in the church of Jesus Christ in South America, Korea, China, Thailand and Africa, is showing increasingly that the knowledge of the glory of the Lord is starting to cover the earth and the sea. Never before in human history has a whole continent so changed in one century. In 1900 the Christian population of Africa was 4%. By the year 2000 it will be 50%! In the light of such events, we can only come to where Habakkuk was advised to be.

> '*The Lord is in his holy temple;*
>   *let all the earth be silent before him.*' (Habakkuk 2:20)

And in the silence Habakkuk's impatient complaint is turned at last into a prayer of adoration and wonder. We come to hear of his attitude, in Habakkuk 3:17 where he says:

> '(**Al**)*though the fig tree does not bud*
>   *and there are no grapes on the vines,*
> *though the olive crop fails*
>   *and the fields produce no food,*
> *though there are no sheep in the pen*
>   *and no cattle in the stalls,*

> *yet I will rejoice in the Lord,*
> *I will be joyful in God my Saviour.'*   (Habakkuk 3:17)

'**Although** the Babylonians come and wreak havoc and vengeance, destroying our land and its people, although they root up the crops and kill all of our animals so that there is nothing but absolute barrenness left, **yet** I will rejoice in the Lord,' Habakkuk says. Here is the attitude in prayer for which God looks in his maturing believer.

Although my children may be sick, although I am lonely and confused, although no one seems to understand me or listen to me, although I may lose my health and my job and my reputation, although as a church worker I may see such little fruit, **yet** will I submit to God and serve him and follow him and trust him and place my faith in him; yet will I honour and praise him. Like Job, even though the Lord slay me, yet will I worship him (Job 13:15). For he alone is God. He alone is King of Kings, Lord of Lords, Prince of Peace, almighty, all merciful, eternal.

It is not '**if**' or '**because**' but '**although**'. He is our God and we are his children. Not '**if**', not '**because**' but '**although**' and we will worship him and pray to him always, come what may.

> ' . . . *Day and night* (the living creatures) *never stop saying:*

> > *"Holy, holy, holy*
> > *is the Lord God Almighty,*
> > *who was, and is, and is to come."*

> *Whenever the living creatures give glory, honour and thanks to him who sits on the throne and who lives for ever and ever, the twenty-four elders fall down before him who sits on the throne, and worship him who lives for ever and ever. They lay their crowns before the throne and say:*

> > *"You are worthy, our Lord and God,*
> > *to receive glory and honour and power,*
> > *for you created all things,*
> > *and by your will they were created*
> > *and have their being."' *   (Revelation 4:8–11)

Endnote

1. Anthony Acknoyd. 'Have I got a life for you!', *Good Weekend*, September 13, 1997, 26.

A Final Word

Some of those who participated in the martyrdom of the Muslim convert (Chapter 7), because of his life and witness, have since become followers of Jesus themselves.

Selected Bibliography

Anderson, Leith. *When God Says No.* Minneapolis, Minnesota: Bethany House Publishers, 1996.

Bright, Vonette and Jennings, Ben A. *Unleashing the Power of Prayer.* Chicago: Moody Press, 1989.

Bryant, David. *Concerts of Prayer.* Ventura, California: Regal Books, 1984.

Cho, Paul Y. *Prayer: Key to Revival.* Herts, England: Word Books, 1985.

Christenson, Evelyn. *What Happens When Women Pray.* Wheaton, Illinois: Victor Books, 1975.

Duewel, Wesley L. *Touch the World Through Prayer.* Grand Rapids, Michigan: Francis Ashbury Press, 1986.

Eastman, Dick. *Change the World School of Prayer.* Penshurst, Australia: World Literature Crusade, 1983.

Eastman, Dick. *No Easy Road.* Grand Rapids, Michigan: Baker Book House, 1971.

Graham, Jim. *Prayer.* London: Scripture Union, 1985.

Lea, Larry. *Could You Not Tarry One Hour?* Altamonte Springs, Florida: Creation House, 1987.

Lea, Larry. *The Hearing Ear.* Altamonte Springs, Florida: Creation House, 1988.

Lewis, C.S. *The Screwtape Letters.* New York: MacMillan, 1969.

Lindsay, Gordon. *Prayer That Moves Mountains*. Dallas: Christ for the Nations Inc., reprint 1984.

Lindsell, Harold. *An Evangelical Theology of Missions*. Grand Rapids, Michigan: Zondervan Publishing House.

McKenna, Breige. *Miracles Do Happen*. London: Pan Books, 1987.

Orr, J. Edwin. *The Flaming Tongue. The Impact of 20th Century Revivals*. Chicago: Moody Press, 1973.

Orr, J. Edwin. *The Second Evangelical Awakening*. London: Marshall, Morgan and Scott, 1955.

Orr, J. Edwin. *The Eager Feet. Evangelical Awakenings 1790–1830*. Chicago: Moody Press, 1975.

Orr, J. Edwin. *The Fervent Prayer. The World Wide Impact of the Great Awakening of 1858*. Chicago: Moody Press, 1974.

Prince, Derek. *Created to Praise*. London: Hodder & Stoughton, 1981.

Prince, Derek. *Shaping History Through Prayer and Fasting*. Fort Lauderdale, Florida: Derek Prince Ministries, 1973.

Robinson, Stuart. *Praying the Price*. Tonbridge, Kent: Sovereign World, 1994.

Sankey, Ira. *My Life and Sacred Songs*, 1906.

Sheikh, Bilquis. *I Dared to Call Him Father*. Eastbourne: Kingsway Publications, 1978.

Shibley, David. *Let's Pray in the Harvest*. Rockwall, Texas: Church on the Rock, 1985.

Torrey, R.A. *The Power of Prayer*. Grand Rapids, Michigan: Zondervan, 1974.

Wagner, C. Peter. *Praying With Power*. Ventura, California: Regal, 1997.

Watson, David. *Fear No Evil*. London: Hodder & Stoughton, 1984.

Whillhite, J. Bob. *Why Pray?* Altamonte Springs, Florida: Creation House, 1988.

Articles

Acknoyd, Anthony. 'Have I got a life for you!'. *Good Weekend*, 13 September 1997, 26.

Allen, R. Earl. 'Quotable'. *Ministries Today*, July/August 1997, 16.

Arndell, R. Seaton. 'Revival and Mission'. *The Australian Baptist*, May 1990, 16, 46, 47.

Cho, David Yonggi. 'My 30-day Battle with Satan'. *Dawn Report*, August 1995, 3–5.

CWR Revival World Report, May/June 1997.

Every Home for Christ, September 1993, 4.

Glen, G.J. 'How Can I Know God's Will in My Life?'. *Australia's New Day*, May 1982, 16.

Gordon, S.D. 'Prayer, the Greatest Thing'. *Australia's New Day*, April 1983, 40.

'Great Men of Prayer'. *Restore*, April 1993, 13.

Greig, Keith. '30 Days Muslim Prayer Focus'. *Newsletter*. Buderim, Queensland, Australia, August 12, 1997.

Hill, Roland J. 'Fasting: A Discipline Ministers Need'. *Ministry*, March 1990, 6–8.

Lescheid, Helen Grace. 'Ten Questions to Ask When Your Prayers are Unanswered'. *Discipleship Journal*, Issue sixty-eight, 1992, 49.

Mahaney, Charles. 'Why Don't I Pray More?'. *Pastoral Renewal*, April 1986, 145–147.

Morrow, Lance. 'Evil'. *Time*, 10 June 1991, 46–51.

O'Connor, Greg. 'Miracles in Cuba'. *New Day*, May 1990, 7–9.

Peters, John. 'David Yonggi-Cho Man of Faith'. *CWR Revival World Report*, November/December 1997, 13.

'Praying Through the Window 111'. *The Unreached Peoples*, The Christian Information Network, Colorado Springs, USA.

Ravenhill, Leonard. 'Give Me Children or I Die'. *CWR Revival World Report*, May/June 1997, 11.

Rogers, Wayman. 'Fasting'. *Church Growth*, December 1988.

Subin, Bhaumik, Meenakshi Ganguly, and Tim McGirk. 'Seeker of Souls'. *Time*, 15 September 1997, 73.

Underwood, Anne, Donna Foote, Claudia Kalb and Brad Stone. 'Is God Listening?'. *Newsweek* (Australian Edition), 1 April, 1997, 63.

Wagner, C. Peter. 'Message from the President'. *AD2000 United Prayer Track Brochure*, nd.

Wagner, C. Peter. 'Spiritual Power in Urban Evangelism: Dynamic Lessons from Argentina'. *Evangelical Missions Quarterly*, 27 April 1991, 132.

Ward, C.M. 'Revival Time Pulpit.' *Sermon Book No. 4*, Springfield, Missouri: Assemblies of God National Radio Department, 1960, 77–79.

White, R.E.O. 'When God Says "No"'. *Australian Baptist*, 25 May 1988, 6.

Wiersbe, Warren. 'Confident Living'. *Good News Broadcasting Association, Inc.*, 1988.

Wilkinson. 'Unanswered Prayer – A Trial of Faith'. *New Life*, 11 March 1993.

Woodward, Kenneth L. 'Is God Listening?'. *Newsweek*, 1 April, 1997, 81.

Primary Source

Dawn Friday – fax, 97/20, via e-mail.

If you have enjoyed this book and would like to help us to send a copy of it and many other titles to needy pastors in the **Third World**, please write for further information or send your gift to:

**Sovereign World Trust
PO Box 777, Tonbridge
Kent TN11 0ZS
United Kingdom**

or to the **'Sovereign World'** distributor in your country.